THE
REAL
BOB PAISLEY

Outside the Paisley Gates,
He said: 'Paisley, they
But you left
Back in Rome
Now it's glory
fields of

I heard a Kopite calling
have taken you away'
a great eleven,
in '77,
round the
Anfield Road

THIS BOOK IS DEDICATED BY THE PAISLEY
FAMILY TO THE SUPPORTERS OF LIVERPOOL
FOOTBALL CLUB, WHO HELPED BOB MAKE
HIS FOOTBALLING DREAMS COME TRUE AND
TO THE CITY OF LIVERPOOL, WHICH HE CAME
TO CALL HOME

THE REAL BOB PAISLEY

ADDITIONAL RESEARCH/WRITING:

KEN ROGERS, JAMES CLEARY, ALAN JEWELL,
GAVIN KIRK, PAUL DOVE

PRODUCTION/DESIGN:

PAUL DOVE, BARRY PARKER

ADDITIONAL PHOTOGRAPHY:

BARRY PARKER

Sport Media
A Trinity Mirror Business

EXECUTIVE EDITOR: KEN ROGERS EDITOR: STEVE HANRAHAN
PRODUCTION EDITOR: PAUL DOVE ART EDITOR: RICK COOKE
SUB EDITOR: ROY GILFOYLE
SALES AND MARKETING MANAGER: ELIZABETH MORGAN
DESIGNERS: BARRY PARKER, COLIN SUMPTER, LEE ASHUN,
GLEN HIND, ALISON GILLILAND, JAMIE DUNMORE, JAMES KENYON
WRITERS: CHRIS MCLOUGHLIN, GAVIN KIRK, DAVID RANDLES,
JOHN HYNES, PAUL HASSALL

PUBLISHED IN GREAT BRITAIN IN 2007 BY: TRINITY MIRROR SPORT MEDIA,
PO BOX 48, OLD HALL STREET, LIVERPOOL L69 3EB.

ISBN 978 1905 266 26 5

MAIN PHOTOGRAPHS: LIVERPOOL DAILY POST AND ECHO, TRINITY MIRROR.
ADDITIONAL IMAGES COURTESY OF THE PAISLEY FAMILY COLLECTION

SPECIAL THANKS FOR THE MAKING OF THIS BOOK GO TO JESSIE & GRAHAM PAISLEY

PRINTED BY BROAD LINK ENTERPRISE LTD

THE REAL BOB PAISLEY
AS TOLD BY
THE PAISLEY FAMILY

CONTENTS

Photographed on board
R.M.S. QUEEN MARY

— FOOTBALL FIRST, WEDDINGS SECOND —
BUT WE NEVER QUESTIONED IT
— SHERWOOD FOREST AND A BAD CASE OF
MISTAKEN IDENTITY
— STAR TURN AT SCHOOL AND PICKING
OUT A TUNE ON THE ORGAN
— MAKING THE MOST OF A FESTIVE
FEAST
— COLLEGE LIFT WITH A BACON BUTTY
AND AN ANFIELD SURPRISE

THE REAL BOB PAISLEY

Foreword

Kenny Dalglish poses for a picture in the Anfield trophy room in August, 1977, after being signed for Liverpool by Bob Paisley

I was more than happy to sign the petition in support of a posthumous knighthood for Bob Paisley which was sent to 10 Downing Street this year.

To me, it's simply an embarrassment to this country that any group of Liverpool fans has had to start a campaign to see him honoured for his outstanding service to football.

He is without doubt the most successful English manager ever. He won six league championships, three European Cups and a UEFA Cup – his record speaks for itself.

When you look at the way honours are thrown around now, to cricket teams for one-off successes and rugby teams who do similar, it enrages me that Bob's achievements and legacy have not yet been properly recognised.

Sir Alex Ferguson and I were rivals, but he was awarded a knighthood on the back of United's European success in Barcelona, and rightly so in my opinion.

What I don't understand is why they would hand out current honours without taking the time to honour those people who have been deserving of the acknowledgment for longer? Personally I can think of no-one more deserving of a knighthood than Bob Paisley.

Bob was an unassuming man, he wasn't interested in self-promotion or media attention. He was at his happiest getting on with his job. I believe that he must have made more than a million decisions over the course of his career and I'll wager now that 99.9 per cent of the decisions he took he got spot on.

He wasn't ever interested in publicity or fame, he wanted those things for his teams and he wanted it through success. He had a simple outlook on life. My abiding memory of him away from the pitch is of a quiet, gentle man in a knitted cardigan, studying the racing form. If his family were healthy, his team was successful and he could get a wee bet on the horses then he was happy. He loved the simple life.

People forget sometimes because of the size of Bill Shankly's personality that Bob was there in the background in the beginning along with Joe Fagan and Ronnie Moran. Without that four who knows where this club would be now.

I will never forget the role he played as an advisor after I took over as manager. He was always there with suggestions and never interested in taking the credit if something he suggested worked.

The night of the Roma game when the fans had a Bob Paisley night in his honour will live with me forever. They brought out some of his trophies at half-time, because they couldn't bring them all out, and Jessie received the most rapturous round of applause. I was moved almost to tears and he deserves every last clap he got that night.

I hope you enjoy reading about Bob Paisley's life, because he is a man with an amazing story to tell.

**KENNY
DALGLISH**

PLAYING
for the team

FEARLESS. HARD-WORKING. COMPETITIVE.
THESE WERE THE QUALITIES THAT MADE
BOB PAISLEY A CROWD FAVOURITE AT ANFIELD
WHEN HE PULLED ON A LIVERPOOL SHIRT

Bulldog Bob – tough tackler and a long throw specialist

1939-1954

The Playing Years

Many fans remember Paisley the manager but he also served the Reds with distinction as a player. It was while plying his trade as a wing-half at Anfield that his leadership qualities came to the fore. He experienced mixed fortunes but his determined displays proved that he had the character to fulfil further senior roles at the club

Bulldog Bob

Local paper, Unknown source, 1947

Left half is where he shines and this season his dour, bulldog-like displays have made him a great favourite. Has won a regular place by sheer dogged tenacity, keen tackling and tireless energy. Is one of the best throw-in experts.

He's a long throw star

**Liverpool Echo,
Jan 16, 1947,
Unknown author**

A new claimant for the title of champion thrower-in from the touchline has come on the scene. He is Bob Paisley, Liverpool's left half-back.

I watched Paisley against Chelsea recently and every time he heaved the ball it flew into play in a Sammy Weaver-like manner; I should say he can throw even farther than the former Newcastle, Chelsea and England star.

Paisley, who uses the long throw with discretion, has had to practise hard to acquire this skill.

Some folk, because of his name, think Paisley is a Scot. Actually he is an Englishman who played in the Bishop Auckland team that won the Amateur Cup in 1938-39.

16 JAN 1947

He's a Long Throw Star

A NEW claimant for the title of champion thrower-in from the touch-line has come on the scene. He is Bob Paisley, Liverpool's left half-back.

I watched Paisley against Chelsea recently, and every time he heaved the ball it flew into play in a Sammy Weaver-like manner: I should say he can throw even farther than the former Newcastle, Chelsea and England star.

Paisley, who uses the long throw with discretion, has had to practise hard to acquire this skill.

Some folk, because of his name, think Paisley is a Scot. Actually he is an Englishman who played in the Bishop Auckland team that won the Amateur Cup in 1938-39.

His tough upbringing turned Paisley into the kind of no-nonsense player that crowds take to their heart

Story Of The Seasons

1937-38
Having excelled for Eppleton Senior Mixed School and Hetton Juniors as a schoolboy star, Bob was forced to bounce back from rejection at an early age. Deemed too small by boyhood favourites Sunderland, Wolves and Tottenham, it would be Bishop Auckland who came to the rescue. The 18-year-old joined prior to the start of the new season, on wages of three shillings and sixpence per match. Bob was fortunate to join such a club though, the Bishops boasting a rich pedigree in non-League circles.

1938-39
The campaign proved to be one of the most successful in Bishop Auckland's history. Paisley was instrumental in helping the club collect a record 10th amateur championship, one of three trophies won that season (including the Amateur Cup). The success is all the more remarkable given that the club at one point were forced to play 13 games in 14 days.

Sunderland suddenly began to show an interest again although they would lose out to Liverpool, their manager George Kay having been given word from Paisley that he would sign for the Anfield club. This he duly did following the Amateur Cup final, for a £25 signing-on fee with wages of £8 a week in season, and £6 during the summer. Two days after the treble was completed (victory over South Shields in the Durham Challenge Cup), on May 8th 1939, Bob boarded a train bound for Liverpool – and the beginning of a memorable relationship.

1939-40
The start of Bob's career didn't bode well for the future. Having played just two reserve games following a tough pre-season, World War Two broke out and suddenly priorities rightly turned away from the football pitch.

The War Years

Paisley made 33 appearances for the club in the North Regional League, scoring 10 goals before being posted abroad in 1941. He would resume his career in 1945-46 when temporary Football League Northern and Southern Divisions were set up although the FA Cup resumed, with a two-legged format introduced for the earlier rounds.

Bob made his official first-team debut against Chester City on January 5th, 1946 at Sealand Road, which saw the Reds claim a 2-0 win. The game saw eight Liverpool players make their debuts, including Billy Liddell and Laurie Hughes, the former scoring the first goal. Despite going through 4-1 on aggregate, a 5-0 defeat at the hands of Bolton Wanderers contributed to a 5-2 defeat over two legs in the following round. Paisley was one of five players who played in all four cup games, while in the league he appeared in another 24 games, scoring two goals.

1946-47

The Football League resumed official matches again, while the FA Cup reverted to its original format. Bob was absent for the opening two games but made his full league debut on September 7th, 1947, against Chelsea at Anfield. Paisley was one of three changes made following the home midweek defeat to Middlesbrough, coming in at No 6 for Eddie Spicer. On a dramatic afternoon, Liverpool claimed a 7-4 victory with the recalled Billy Liddell (also making his league debut), Willie Fagan and Bill Jones all scoring twice.

The honeymoon ended four days later, as former Anfield favourite Matt Busby, now in charge of Manchester United, helped guide his new club to a 5-0 victory. The defeat persuaded the Reds to part with a club-record £12,500 for Newcastle United's Albert Stubbins and he made a scoring debut in the 3-1 defeat of Bolton Wanderers, just seven days after Paisley's debut against Chelsea. Including the Trotters match, Liverpool embarked on a 12-match unbeaten run, a sequence which saw Jack Balmer score hat-tricks in three successive ▶

**Sport As I See It
by Leslie Edwards,
Liverpool Evening Express**

November 1, 1948

When they elect the Footballer of the Year at the end of the season, they will doubtless choose some much publicised figure, glamorous for a succession of caps and other football brilliancies which seem to count for all today.

It will surprise me if they so much as mention the name Robert Paisley (Liverpool) but if they did it would be the finest tribute to the vast mass of club players. For this reason: Paisley in a football sense is one of those players who gives his all till it hurts. Even then he refused to lie down and be treated as casualties usually are.

Struck on the side of the head and concussed by a tremendous shot by Dodgin, early in the match at Newcastle Paisley was knocked unconscious, but resumed at outside-left. Ten minutes before the interval, he was so shaky trainer Shelley had to carry him off.

During the interval the unusual method of walking him up and down outside the

telling off from Dad!

games (still a top-flight record) –
a sequence which included 15
goals in seven games.

Consistency proved key and
with Paisley making 33
appearances at left-half (Spicer
would replace him for the other
nine games at wing-half),
Liverpool claimed the First
Division title for only a fifth time.
Fixture congestion meant the
Championship wasn't decided
until June 14th, with title-
challenging Stoke City's defeat at
Sheffield United handing the Reds
the title. Liverpool's final game
had been at Wolves two weeks
before on May 31st, a 2-1 victory.
Little did Paisley know that the
same ground would provide
similar happy memories nearly 30
years later.

Incidentally, Bob was, at 5 feet
7 and a half inches, the smallest
member of the Championship-
winning side by some two and a
half inches. Paisley also made six
appearances in the FA Cup, as
Liverpool reached the semi-final,
losing to Burnley in a replay.

Of that season, Paisley recalled
in a 1979 Liverpool Echo series:
"We had some good lads in that
side. I remember the skipper was
Jack Balmer, here was the sprint
champion Jim Harley, Cyril
Sidlow, Laurie Hughes, Bill Jones,
Phil Taylor and then in came
Albert Stubbins – for the huge fee
in those days of £12,500.

"There were only two
competitions to go for then – the
Cup and the League – and there
was nothing like the number of
games we have now. There was
plenty of pressure of course,
trying to win these competitions,
but nothing like the lads are
subjected to today."

1947-48
The champions defended their
title with a whimper, rather than
with style. A poor start to the
campaign dampened expectations
of a third back-to-back First
Division success, while a poor run
in the new year signalled the very
real threat of relegation, come
March (a run of six successive
defeats included four consecutive
3-0 reverses in league and cup
games), the Reds eventually
finishing 11th.

main grandstand was used in the hope that
he would 'come to'.

Having seen this, I was amazed when,
nine minutes after the match had restarted,
Paisley trotted on again to do useful work
at outside-left before trying to head a goal
off a Liddell centre and falling unconscious
for a second time. Again he was carried off.

Last night, from Newcastle hospital, he
sounded rather subdued but was still
inclined to be as chirpy as usual. X-ray
examination of his head, yesterday,
satisfied the specialist that all was well.

And this main piece of news was
something that Paisley asked me to relay to
his wife in Liverpool as soon as possible.

Today there will be more x-rays – this
time of the shoulder and the neck, which
is still very stiff and painful – and then,
all being well, this most likeable little
character will be looking for the first train
home.

"I remember nothing except the first
ten minutes," he told me last night.

"When I 'came to' first I was dressed
and my father, who had been at the
match, was angry with me for going on a
second time and for daring to head the
ball again.

"It was hard work convincing him I did
not even remember coming back, much
less trying to score!"

Despite the team's struggles, Paisley enjoyed his best season yet, playing 37 times in the league (twice in the FA Cup) and scoring his first senior goal for the club, against Wolves on the final day of the season on May 1st, 1948.

1948-49

Liverpool came into the season determined to improve, although they would end up finishing a place lower in the league. Stubbins missed most of the season and the team relied heavily on Balmer and Liddell. Paisley played 36 times in the league and another four in the FA Cup, scoring once at Portsmouth in a 3-2 defeat in April 1949.

1949-50

After the relative disappointment in the previous two seasons, the club made a record-breaking start to 1949-50. Liverpool went 19 league games unbeaten (a mark broken by Leeds United in 1973-74), but after losing their first game at Huddersfield Town on December 10th, they would finish only 8th. In the FA Cup, however, following a quarter-final defeat of Blackpool, the Reds were drawn to face neighbours Everton at Manchester City's Maine Road.

With Paisley in the side, Liverpool secured a 2-0 triumph with the man himself lobbing the opener in the first half. It helped book a Cup final place for the first time in 36 years.

Unfortunately for Bob, an injury in the weeks leading up to the final persuaded the board (who picked the side) to leave him out of the team to face Arsenal at Wembley – despite assurances he was fully recovered. In at half-back were England players Laurie Hughes and Bill Jones. His team-mates went down 2-0 to the Gunners, although Paisley did receive a runners-up medal after the club asked the FA to produce a special medal for him.

1950-51

Paisley would recover from the heartache of the previous season to play in all but one league

Top: An aerial battle in the Main Stand car park and (right) a lap of honour at Anfield after losing the 1950 FA Cup final

'WHEN PEOPLE TALK OF THEIR DARKEST DAY, THAT WAS MINE. I READ THAT I WOULDN'T BE PLAYING IN A NEWSPAPER AND THE BOTTOM FELL OUT OF MY WORLD. I HAD BEEN A REGULAR AND PLAYING WELL ... AND THEN TRAGEDY STRUCK'

The cruel FA Cup snub that taught me to bite my tongue and sleep on it

By Bob Paisley

(From a Liverpool Echo series 'The Amazing Bob Paisley' by Horace Yates in 1979)

If you had a safe place in the League, life was a piece of cake. In 1949-50 we looked like winning the League again, and at one stage went 19 games unbeaten, which remained a record for a long time, but instead of winning the League we went to Wembley to play Arsenal in the FA Cup final.

Even now I cringe a bit when I think of it, not just because we lost 2-0, but because I lost my place. When people talk of their darkest day, that was mine. I read that I wouldn't be playing in a newspaper, and the bottom fell out of my world.

I had been a regular and playing well. I scored one of the goals that helped to beat Everton in the semi-final. Then tragedy struck. I got a knee injury.

We had two international centre halves, Bill Jones and Laurie Hughes. Before the final they were both chosen for England, one in the 'B' team, and I expect that put the directors under some pressure.

I was never big-headed and had never taken it for granted that I would be picked, but it was a knockout blow all the same.

Wembley was the event of the season, probably even more so than it is today. Anybody who could kick a ball wanted to kick it at Wembley.

I was offered what was big money in those days to pour out my heart to a newspaper.

Thankfully I thought better of it. I suppose it taught me a lesson that first thoughts are not always wisest. Often it is better to sleep on a problem.

That was the only occasion in my lifetime when I was disenchanted with Liverpool. I have lived to bless the day when I bit my tongue and said nothing.

I didn't want to move really, and I reasoned it out that a similar sort of thing could easily happen somewhere else. Championships to Liverpool in those days were not the be-all and end-all of a season. Naturally they would win it if they could, but they were a very popular club socially, and there was no real concern so long as we maintained a respectable position.

I continued to play until the 1953-54 season, the year Liverpool were relegated. That was a blow to our pride, but it so happened that the whole of my professional career was spent in the First Division.

The 35-year-old Paisley retired at the end of the 1953-54 season and considered returning to the bricklaying trade. However, the board offered him a job on the backroom staff having impressed over the years with his analytical mind. He had also studied a correspondence course in physiotherapy and was taken on as reserve-team coach. It was to be the start of big things to come.

game (only Eddie Spicer would play in every game), becoming club captain in the process. His one goal came against West Brom in a 1-1 draw at Anfield in March.

It would be a season of some upheaval, with George Kay stepping down as manager in February, to be replaced by Don Welsh. Liverpool would finish in the top half in ninth, although they fell at the first hurdle in the FA Cup, 3-1 at Norwich City.

1951-52
Under the captaincy of Paisley, Liverpool would finish 11th in the table although they were now renowned more as a mid-table outfit. Paisley made 40 league and cup appearances (only Liddell and Kevin Baron made more), scoring a career-best three goals. One came in the FA Cup fourth-round victory over Wolves, with the others scored against West Brom (3-3 draw) and Stoke City (2-1 win).

1952-53
A 2-0 Anfield victory over Chelsea on the final day of the season saved the Reds from relegation to the Second Division, although the finishing position of 17th covered few of the squad with glory. Paisley played in only 26 games, scoring twice against Newcastle United (5-3) and Portsmouth (3-1) although he did feature in that final game.

1953-54
Having failed to yield the warnings of the previous campaign, Liverpool crashed out of the First Division, finishing rock bottom.

They yielded only 28 points despite scoring 68 goals – the problem was at the other end, letting in 97 – the worst tally in the Football League. Paisley played in 19 games, again scoring two goals in consecutive games against Sheffield Wednesday (2-2) and Aston Villa (6-1).

His final appearance came in the 3-1 defeat to Sheffield United at Bramall Lane on March 13th, 1954.

Pulling TOGETHER

BOB PAISLEY MASTERMINDED AN UNHERALDED PERIOD OF ANFIELD SUCCESS. THIS IS THE STORY OF THE OTHER TEAM THAT HELPED MAKE IT ALL HAPPEN – HIS FAMILY

It was the spring of 1954 when Liverpool star Bob Paisley received the news every player dreads – he was getting released by his club. The future looked bleak at first but he was soon to receive a job offer that would set him and Liverpool on a long and winding road to success . . .

Phil Taylor, Bill Jones, Paisley not retained by club

Liverpool Evening Express, May 4, 1954

Liverpool FC today provided several surprises when they issued their retained list of players for the coming season. Among the notable absentees are:

Bill Jones – the captain who has has 15 years at the club. Play-anywhere type.

Phil Taylor – former captain, one of the classiest half-backs the club has ever had.

Bobby Paisley – the tough little North Easterner who specialises in the long throw and is of the never-say-die order.

Eddie Spicer – one of the unluckiest players in the country. Has twice broken his leg and is not expected to play again.

My Bob: Warcry

FAMILY FOREWORD

IT was September 1st, 1997. The Liverpool Former Players Association were staging their annual dinner at Liverpool's Crowne Plaza Hotel, commemorating 20 years since the Reds won the European Cup for the first time under the legendary Bob Paisley, the glory that was Rome '77.

It was an incredible turn-out. Of course, the great man had died on February 14th, 1996. It was left to his wife Jessie to speak on his behalf and she wasn't going to disappoint the sons of Anfield who were out in force to remember arguably the greatest night in Liverpool's history. The room was packed to the rafters with fans and they gave Jessie an emotional welcome. Slightly frail, but as feisty as ever, she stepped in front of the microphone and gave a speech that brought tears to the eyes of everyone.

More than that she had players and supporters in the palm of her hand as she spoke with incredible passion, talking about 'My Bob' and letting fly about the way it was and the way it is. In a nutshell, she reminded people that when Bob Paisley won his three European Cups, you didn't get a second chance in a group stage if you lost a match or even two. With the room absolutely silent in a show of absolute respect, Jessie opened her heart . . .

I didn't travel to Rome in 1977. I sat at home with my daughter-in-law and a friend and we watched it on television. On the final whistle I suddenly saw Bob jump in the air and I'd never seen him do that before.

He was normally so placid, but this said everything.

He was never one for shouting or going over the top, but this was so special, to him, the club and the fans. There he was going absolutely mad and we couldn't get over it. We were so proud.

When the lads came home the next day, they took me to meet him at the airport. I was the first one to spot him coming off the plane and it was so exciting, but it was nothing like what happens now.

I'll tell you what we did. We came home, had a cup of tea and went to bed! Bob would have already been thinking about the next one.

I'll tell you something about my Bob. He won the European Cup three times in the days when each country only provided one club for the competition – the champions.

The only other way in was if you had won the trophy the year before.

> 'HE WAS NEVER ONE FOR SHOUTING OR GOING OVER THE TOP, BUT THIS WAS SO SPECIAL, TO HIM, THE CLUB AND THE FANS. THERE HE WAS GOING ABSOLUTELY MAD AND WE COULDN'T GET OVER IT. WE WERE SO PROUD'

from the heart

Speech: Jessie talked passionately about Bob's Anfield legacy

There were no little leagues, no second chances like you have now, You were either in or you were out, which was a lot harder. It was as simple as that.

That is why what Bob achieved was so special. He won the European Cup two years on the run, in Rome and at Wembley.

I went to see them win it at Wembley and I went again to Paris in 1981. I travelled there by train and hovercraft – I hated flying. You could say I was one of the original WAGS, but we did it our way.

Bob loved Liverpool FC.

He lived for his job. I'm so proud that he will never be forgotten.

The roar that followed Jessie's speech matched anything that was heard at the Olympic Stadium in 1977. She had struck a chord with a point that was absolutely right. Bob Paisley's achievement in winning three European Cups really was something very special. The most modest manager in football had taken on the real Champions of Europe and triumphed superbly.

His feats will never be forgotten.

❯ **I wondered what on earth I was going to do**

Taken from a tribute by Ian Hargraves in the Liverpool Echo in 1992, Bob Paisley explained his feelings after he was released by the club in 1954:

"In the spring of 1954, several of the older players including Bill Jones, Jackie Balmer and myself were told we would not be retained for the following season.

"I was living in a club house with a wife and two kiddies and I wondered what on earth I was going to do. I had finished my time as a bricklayer's apprentice but the thought of going back to that didn't really appeal so I was delighted when the president, Mr TV Williams, asked if I would like to become the first team trainer.

"The money was less than I had been getting but it meant keeping a job in football and I wasted no time at all in accepting.

"I didn't know anything at all about training so I thought I should find out everything I could and asked Mr Williams if he could use his connections with Littlewoods founder Sir John Moores to help me obtain an introduction to the Liverpool hospitals so I could see how patients were dealt with.

"At that time there was very little science in the treatment of injured players, who could normally accept no more than verbal encouragement and a cold sponge applied to the back of the neck. It was amazing how quickly the sight of the sponge would make some of them recover!"

Don't call on me unless you've got double pneumonia!

Sport As I See It by Leslie Edwards: Liverpool Daily Post, August 31, 1956

Most apt remark of the week? Bob Paisley's to members of his Reserve side at Anfield: "Don't call me on the field to attend to

❯

you unless you've got double pneumonia!"

The explanation is not, as one would suppose, that Paisley is asking the side he trains to be as tough on the field as he was, but that he is suffering from an old ankle injury which makes running impossible!

Paisley's post

Liverpool Evening Express, By Ranger, 1954

Following on the announcement yesterday of the appointment of Phil Taylor as full-time coach to Liverpool FC, news is released today of a second Anfield appointment – that of Bob Paisley as trainer to the Central League side.

PAISLEY'S POST

Following on the announcement yesterday of the appointment of Phil Taylor as full-time coach to Liverpool F.C., news is released to-day of a second Anfield appointment—that of Bob Paisley as trainer to the Central League side.

Paisley, like Taylor, has been one of Liverpool's stalwarts throughout all the post-war years, and at the end of last season was placed on the open-to-transfer list at a nominal fee.

Now, after second thoughts, he follows in the footsteps of Jimmy Seddon, who has had charge of the Central League side for the past 15 years. He follows a sound man who has given Liverpool good

Bob Paisley

service. The club will get good service, too, for Paisley, who, apart from his football ability, is just the type for behind-the-scenes work.

Paisley, like Taylor, has been one of Liverpool's stalwarts throughout all the post-war years and at the end of last season was placed on the open-to-transfer list at a nominal fee.

Now, after second thoughts, he follows in the footsteps of Jimmy Seddon, who has had charge of the Central League side for the past 15 years. He follows a sound man who has given Liverpool good service.

GRAHAM'S STORY

BACK in the Swinging Sixties, Liverpool was the centre of the universe, world famous for two things . . . football and the Beatles. There is a remarkable link between Bob and the Beatles in the shape of St. Peter's Church which is situated in the green belt fringe of Liverpool's southern suburb of Woolton. Here, Eleanor Rigby died in the church and was buried along with her name. Nobody came.

Within feet of the subject matter of Lennon and McCartney's haunting hit, Bob Paisley is also buried. The sons and daughters of Liverpool and the entire football family of Britain mourned the loss of a soccer giant who never courted the limelight, but who stamped an indelible mark on all things Anfield as a top class player, trainer, coach, assistant to the legendary Shanks and then manager who would win three European Cups.

Bob and the Beatles are also inextricably linked because through St. Peter's a musical phenomenon was born in the church hall just across the road. This was where Paul first met John, after watching him perform with his group The Quarrymen. By coincidence, St. Peter's was the family church of the Paisley family and it remains central in their lives. Bob's middle son Graham, a former banker, works there on a daily basis as Church Administrator, responsible for the day to day running of the building.

As quietly spoken and modest as his famous father, he rarely if ever reveals his link to a legend when pilgrims come to the church to find Eleanor Rigby, talk about the Beatles and enquire about Bob Paisley's final resting place.

Modest: Graham in historic St. Peter's Church Hall, Woolton

It's moving when they ask to see Dad's grave – his name lives on

The Paisley Years
IN HEADLINES

> The club will get good service, too, for Paisley, who, apart from his football ability, is just the type for behind-the-scenes work, for his cheery personality keeps everybody happy and contented.
>
> Paisley was signed by the late George Kay from Bishop Auckland in May, 1939 and his wholehearted and determined displays made him a warm favourite with the crowd.

Liverpool's managerial decision

From newspaper cutting, May 1, 1957

At their weekly board meeting last night Liverpool FC directors appointed Mr Phil Taylor as manager. Hitherto he has been acting-manager only.

While Mr Taylor has been acting manager, the club did not fill the coaching position which he formerly occupied.

They have now appointed Bob Paisley, at present second-team trainer, as chief coach. He will take up the duties when the players report for training next season.

There was a big difference in the styles of play of Phil Taylor and Bob Paisley; the one stylish and thoughtful; the other rugged and determined. If they work in double harness in such a way as to bring the best out of the player in the same directions Liverpool should benefit considerably. Here's wishing both of them the best of luck.

An undertaking from Paisley

Liverpool Echo, October 19, 1966

Liverpool trainer Bob Paisley was yesterday ordered by the Football Association Disciplinary Committee to give an undertaking to the Football Association within seven days not to repeat the action for which he was reported in the Aston Villa-Liverpool

I'm very much like dad in that I'm quietly spoken and consider myself a modest type. It's the way he brought us up.

It's quite moving when visitors come to the church and ask me to show them where Bob Paisley is buried. Of course, I would never say who I am.

My mum Jessie always brought us here as a family. Of course, dad would be working on Sundays. He would always go into Anfield to treat the players who had been injured the day before. It was probably a day when he would also sit with Bill Shankly and they would begin to discuss the previous day's action.

When he retired in 1983, Dad was finally able to come here more regularly. It's a lovely church with a remarkable history. Liverpool remains famous for the Beatles and football and it's all here. We get loads of interest and I'm naturally proud of my father's link.

league game on October 1.

At the time, he was booked by the referee, Paisley was attending to an injury to Roger Hunt and it is thought the referee overheard a remark intended only for the ears of the player.

A trainer looks for the faults

Liverpool Echo, September 23, 1967

In an article talking about how he helps to manage the Liverpool squad, he was asked about which careers his two sons – boys of 19 and 17 – would follow ...

"Both the boys are fervent Liverpool fans," he said. "They come to all our games at Anfield and see a lot of the away matches as well but neither of them will be going into football as a career.

"In any case, they haven't got the ability," he added in his forthright way.

My choice from three cup final sides

Liverpool Daily Post, April 28, 1971

As part of the build-up to the 1971 FA Cup final, Paisley was asked to name his best eleven from the last three sides to reach Wembley in the competition.

His choice was: Clemence (71), Lawler (71), Smith (65/71), Yeats (65), Byrne (65), Taylor (50), Hall (71), St John (65), Hunt (65), Stubbins (50), Liddell (50).

Bob's back and wants revenge

Liverpool Daily Post, April 30, 1971

Ahead of the Reds' meeting with Arsenal at Wembley in 1971, Paisley looked back on the biggest disappointment of his professional career – being dropped for the 1950 FA Cup final.

Dad won three European Cups – and every game he played with us!

Paisley treble: Me, Robert and Christine

Dad adored Mum and they had three children – me, Robert and Christine who in turn would go on to provide him with seven grandchildren who he idolised.

He doted on his grandchildren – Helen, Rachael, Jane, Julie, Carol, Kirsty and his only grandson Stuart. It's strange, but Bill Shankly's family was also dominated by girls. Dad loved it when the children were about. My eldest daughter Helen was his first grandchild. She was born in 1979 by which time three Championships and two European Cups were already in the bag. She was the one who knew him best, but he loved them all. I would smile when I watched him playing with them.

When we were kids he would never let us win in any game because he was so competitive. He had mellowed a bit with his grandchildren and they could nearly get round him, but dad was always a winner.

My brother Robert was the eldest. My sister Chris was the youngest.

We moved to Woolton when I was two and before that we lived in

Early days: With Dad and older brother Robert in 1950

"It was the most sickening thing in my life. It is every player's ambition to play in a Cup final at Wembley and I had played in every round up to the final.

"I always wore the no.6 shirt and for the first time since our Cup run started, both Laurie Hughes and Bill Jones, who were both centre-halves, were fit.

"Throughout the earlier rounds, first one had been injured and then the other one came in and just as the first was getting fit again, the other would be injured.

"To complicate matters, they had both been picked for the England teams. Bill Jones had been picked for England A and Laurie Hughes for England B.

"I think it was those representative honours going their way which finally cost me a Cup final place.

"In my opinion, they took the coward's way out by selecting Laurie Hughes at centre-half and Bill Jones at left-half. It meant they were not creating a hue and cry by leaving an international out of the side. They left me out instead – and I considered then, and still think now, I was the best man in that position."

Shankly's new contract

Liverpool Daily Post, July 9, 1971

Bill Shankly, happier than at any stage of his Anfield career, has agreed a new three-year contract with Liverpool – with the option of extending it to five years.

This was one of a series of appointments announced last night, when Bob Paisley, who has served Liverpool as player and trainer since 1939, stepped up to the role of assistant to the manager.

'WHEN WE WERE KIDS HE WOULD NEVER LET US WIN IN ANY GAME BECAUSE HE WAS SO COMPETITIVE. HE HAD MELLOWED A BIT WITH HIS GRANDCHILDREN AND THEY COULD NEARLY GET ROUND HIM, BUT DAD WAS ALWAYS A WINNER'

Second team trainer Joe Fagan, with a hat-trick of Central League successes to commend his efforts, takes over as first team trainer and former club skipper and left back Ronnie Moran steps up to become trainer to the Central League side.

Reuben Bennett is now assigned to special duties, which will probably include assessing opponents and reporting on recommended players.

Talking of the changes, Shankly said: "We are trying to build an impregnable fortress here – and we are nearly there."

Paisley saves tennis star

July 13, 1971

After treatment by Bob Paisley, assistant to Liverpool FC manager Bill Shankly, last night Bob Hewitt (South Africa), no. 1 seed in Rothman's North of England lawn tennis championships at Hoylake, had his fears removed that he might not be able to continue.

Hewitt has Achilles tendon trouble but after strapping it, Paisley said: "I think he will get through it alright. The tendon is not as inflamed as I had expected.

"I have arranged to see him again on Wednesday, which is a free day for him, and I will take along one of the club's portable treatment machines.

"They have been away for servicing but we should have them back by Wednesday.

"I think the electrical treatment will do him good, although the only real cure is rest."

The Legend's Lieutenants

Liverpool Daily Post, April 26, 1974

In the build-up to another FA Cup final, the Daily Post interviewed manager Bill Shankly on the men

Rare holiday: Together on a boating break on the Thames in 1966

Greystone Road, Broadgreen, in a club house, close to former stars like Billy Liddell and Bill Jones. Mum, who was a teacher, was always the one who was in charge at home. Dad was the quieter one. He was a lovely father, but when we used to play games that focus on winning that part of his professional life always came out.

We would play football up the back pathway at home and he would promise us threepence if we scored a goal past him. We never got our money!

Dad was also an excellent cricketer in the days when Liverpool and Everton would put out a joint team in the summer. He once played in an an exhibition game with famous West Indian Leary Constantine which he was very proud of. When we played cricket up the path, he would spin balls at us that were totally unplayable and smile when he claimed another wicket! He was always a winner.

We had this half-size snooker table at mum's house. I was never very good at it early on and he would give me a points start when we played on a Sunday evening. That had traditionally been the only time he was regularly in because of his

in his backroom team.

"Football is basically a simple game," he said. "Equally, choice of men is not a difficult thing either. Honest and mutual trust are the top of my list, confident of course, of the ability to discharge the duties I have in mind.

"I emphasised that there was to be nothing underhand, no backbiting. Bob Paisley became my assistant. There are so many things to do that a manager must delegate some functions, always confident that everything will be done exactly as they would had he personally directed them.

"I couldn't have found a better man than Bob. He has done a first class job behind the scenes.

"I never had any doubts. I had known him for years as a player and he has given me the same intense loyalty he gave to the club in his playing days."

The obvious choice

Liverpool Daily Post, July 20, 1974

Now it's all over bar the announcement – Bob Paisley is to take over as manager of Liverpool Football Club from Bill Shankly.

That's my reading of the situation as it stands now and as Brian Clough is equally certain to succeed Don Revie as Leeds United manager, both teams will step out for the Charity Shield final, on August 10, in the charge of new managers.

To my knowledge, Paisley has been the only name given any serious consideration and it was because of this that applications for the post were never considered.

Paisley professed complete surprise last night. "The board knew all along that I was prepared to accept any role they desired me to take, whether as manager or assistant to some other manager. That is still the position so long as the conditions are satisfactory. If I am asked to take over, the routine of the club would not change one iota."

football commitments. As my snooker ability began to improve, so the points advantage he gave me began to diminish.

I was soon on a par with him. It had always been the best of three frames, but when my improvement saw me taking a two frame lead it would go up to a five frame match. We would play on until he won. Later, I heard about the five-a-side games at Melwood that Dad and Bill Shankly would organise, always playing on until they got a goal in front. I realised where that determination came from. Even in retirement, when the Alzheimer's was

beginning to set in and affect his memory, he never forgot the importance of coming out on top. That will to win never left him.

When we were kids I can only remember going on one holiday with both mum and dad. Mum was devoted to her teaching. Dad was totally committed to his football. Holidays never coincided. I think a boating holiday on the Thames was the one time we were together for a week, but we never thought of it as a hardship.

Mum was totally supportive of my dad. It was the only way it could have worked.

Dad offered me a trial at Melwood but said: 'You'll never make it!'

Almost exactly 20 years after Paisley had found himself released by the club, he was offered the opportunity to become manager. July of 1974 saw Bill Shankly rock the football world by retiring as Liverpool boss, despite being begged to reconsider the decision by his right-hand man.

"I suggested Bill should take a rest – the last thing I wanted was to have to take his place. I just wanted Bill to carry on and did everything I could to persuade him to change his mind."

One of Shankly's last acts was to recommend Bob as his No 1 choice to take over the reigns, and the board made the wise decision to act on Shankly's words – despite initial reluctance from the man, by then age 55, who would surpass all expectations.

Bob had been with Shankly since the Scot joined the club from Huddersfield Town in December 1959, and upon his appointment he remarked:

"It's like being given the Queen Elizabeth to steer in a force 10 gale."

Few would foresee the glittering times ahead, as Paisley claimed an unprecedented haul of 19 major trophies in only nine years.

Marching into Shankly's shoes

Liverpool Daily Post, July 27, 1974

Two weeks of speculation were ended last night when the annual meeting of Liverpool Football Club heard Bob Paisley named as the club's new manager.

It's a job many have already labelled 'Mission Impossible'.

As Shankly's running-mate for 15 years, Paisley says: "Nobody could have greater respect and admiration for the boss and I would be failing him if after all that time I could not plunge into this task with confidence.

I was a reasonable amateur footballer as a kid. I played for my local school set-up Quarry Bank, but Dad was not one for standing and watching.

He would come for ten to fifteen minutes and then would disappear. I would be 12 or 13 at the time.

He knew I was getting quite keen on the game and I was delighted one day when he suddenly said: 'You are welcome to come for a trial at Melwood.'

That smile soon disappeared when he added: 'But I'll tell you now. You'll never make it!' before telling me: 'You're okay defending, but you can't go forward.'

I played centre-back or full-back but I was under no illusions about my ability. Dad's assessment kept my feet on the ground.

He was just matter of fact about it which, I suppose, is the way he dealt with the professionals around him at Anfield.

Team snap: Wearing the Quarry Bank school colours. I am on the top row, far right – next to Tom Saunders' son Dave. Robert is the keeper, also on the back row

Football mad: Kitted out with Robert in the back garden.
Behind is one of Dad's creations – a home-made 'conservatory'

'I PLAYED CENTRE-BACK OR
FULL-BACK BUT I WAS UNDER NO
ILLUSIONS ABOUT MY ABILITY.
DAD'S ASSESSMENT KEPT MY FEET
ON THE GROUND . . . WHICH I
SUPPOSE IS THE WAY HE DEALT
WITH THE PROFESSIONALS'

> "I will probably never be able to equal the wonderful relationship he has always enjoyed with the crowd but I do claim that I will be his equal in loyalty and dedication.

Marching confidently into Shankly's shoes

"I have always had and always will have every bit as great a hunger for trophies and thirst for success as he has. I am not the least overawed by the size of the job.

"Routines don't change and Bill has always been a boss who believed in allowing his staff to use their own talents.

"He has interfered only rarely and quite honestly, I don't think he has had much to complain about. We have always had a great team behind the team at Anfield. That's the way I shall try to keep it. You don't play around with ideas that have proved to work. You just feed and water them."

Keegan: FA chief to quiz Reds

Liverpool Echo, August 13, 1974

The 1974 Charity Shield was still technically Bill Shankly's last game in charge of Liverpool.

After the match, Paisley officially took over as manager and his first job was to deal with the FA investigation into a Wembley bust-up between Leeds' Billy Bremner and Kevin Keegan.

Paisley said: "These incidents with Kevin Keegan have tended to hide the fact that the team has played some excellent football in our pre-season matches.

"I'm convinced that plenty of notice in the papers for the players, particularly at this pre-season stage, helps to get them motivated.

"I've always regarded it as an important part of the preparations for the season.

"But the managerial changes at Anfield have dominated the scene so much that our players have had to take second place. It is understandable but I'm still sorry that it has been so because it is the players who matter. I hope now from today that the players will take centre stage. Without them, the club is nothing."

New roles for Fagan and Moran

Liverpool Daily Post, August 14, 1974

Bob Paisley's promotion has been achieved without the slightest ripple of upset in the Liverpool camp.

This week, chairman John Smith and his board are likely to rubber stamp Bob's first restructuring moves.

He has recommended promotion for trainer Joe Fagan to the position of coach, with reserve team trainer Ronnie Moran moving up to first team duties.

In Mr Shankly's reign, Liverpool always operated a three-man touchline team and this is a fixture Paisley is anxious to continue.

Moreover, he will be a touchline manager, believing it necessary to keep in the closest touch with events on the field.

1974-75

Apprentice Bob learns the hard way

Paisley's first full season at the helm failed to yield any silverware, a concern noted by fans and media alike following the Shankly years. It would prove to be the only campaign when Paisley won nothing.

The Championship race went right down to the wire, with Dave Mackay guiding Derby County to

Black toe and life

I remember coming home from Quarry Bank school after a match in which someone had stood on my toe which was really bruised. Dad called it 'black toe' and I was soon accompanying him to Anfield for my first ever 'professional' treatment which was quite exciting in its own way because it meant I could go into the Boot Room under the old Paddock.

It was a Sunday and Bill Shankly was already there when we arrived.

They looked at my 'black toe' and suddenly a darning needle was heating up on an old gas ring. I was watching this getting hotter and hotter as dad and Bill talked casually about football.

The next thing I was called to the treatment table and looked away as dad set about relieving the pressure and the pain in my 'black toe' with this basic medical procedure. It worked, but I wondered how many star players had complained about

at the 'sharp' end

their second title in four years, overcoming strong competition from the Reds, who finished two points behind (two points for a win) while Ipswich Town, Everton, Stoke City, Sheffield United and Middlesbrough were also in contention late on in the season. Paisley commented: "I was like an apprentice that ran wide at the bends."

Changes saw youngster Jimmy Case make his debut, while Phil Neal (Paisley's first signing) and Terry McDermott were brought in from Northampton Town and Newcastle United respectively, the duo making their debut in the Merseyside derby at Goodison Park in November (a 0-0 draw). Another new boy was Ray Kennedy – Shankly's last signing while Larry Lloyd joined Coventry City – Paisley's first official deal.

Fourth round defeats in the FA Cup (1-0 at Ipswich Town) and the League Cup (at home to Middlesbrough) were supplemented by further disappointment in Europe. Hungarian outfit Ferencvaros went through in the Cup Winners' Cup on the away goals rule after drawing 1-1 at Anfield and then 0-0 at home. The previous round had seen Liverpool defeat Norway's Strømsgodset 11-0 at Anfield which remains the club's record victory. In that game only Brian Hall and keeper Ray Clemence failed to find the target.

There was success for one squad member though, as Ian Callaghan was named Footballer of the Year by the Football Writers' Association, the veteran missing only one game all season. Ray Clemence and Emlyn Hughes were the other two ever-presents.

Paisley gets the Anfield treatment!

Liverpool Echo, September 4, 1974

Liverpool manager Bob Paisley, the expert at running the Anfield treatment room, is a patient there now!

'black toe' without realising they were inviting the darning needle treatment.

That was the first time I had seen my dad and Bill Shankly together. Their conversation was totally football-based and highlighted their passion for the game. Bill was really friendly, but always totally immersed in the game. Like my dad, he didn't really socialise with anyone outside of football. The common bond was football.

All through my own amateur football career, I got this medical advice from dad whenever I had a problem. I would limp into the house and he would take what would appear to be a cursory glance before dismissing most of the injuries as not serious. One day was slightly different. He declared that I had a fractured tibia and I immediately thought I would be off to hospital.

Dad added that it was a stress fracture and that it would take four

He was involved in an accident yesterday in which his car was in collision with a petrol tanker. The car was badly damaged and he was thrown forward, fortunately without serious injury. But he feels stiff around the neck and shoulders today and is having treatment from coach Joe Fagan.

He said: "I saw the club doctor and I'll be alright. I'll have to take things easily for a few days but it won't keep me off duty."

Paisley: Let's forget the matter

Liverpool Echo, November 7, 1974

"Let's forget it. We don't want to win trophies that way," was how Liverpool manager Bob Paisley announced that he would take no action regarding the bottle throwing incident in Budapest.

Tommy Smith alleged that he had been struck on the shoulder and felled by an empty brandy bottle thrown by a spectator during the closing minutes of the European Cup Winners Cup tie with Ferencvaros, which Liverpool lost on the away goals rule.

Now's the time to act – Paisley

Liverpool Echo, December 9, 1974

Not everything went according to plan in Paisley's first season in the Anfield hotseat.

After a disappointing home draw to Derby County, he warned that he was poised to make changes to the team.

He said: "It's the crowd I feel sorry for because they are as frustrated as the players, who are affected by the atmosphere generated from the terraces.

"I took over an established side when I became manager. I have tried not to disturb that side, to give everyone a fair crack of the whip, to keep faith with them, to give them a vote of confidence.

"I have leaned over backwards

to six weeks to heal. He said there was no point going for an x-ray because the fracture would only show up when the injury was starting to heal. We actually went to the hospital six weeks later and, sure enough, an x-ray showed a healing stress fracture.

After school, I went on to play for Quarry Bank Old Boys in the Zingari League. It would be the beginning of the Seventies.

It was strange in a way. I would get ribbed about being Bob Paisley's son. The lads would joke that I should be able to play better, but many of them were passionate Liverpudlians and I really enjoyed my football at that level.

In those days, the kits were very different to what they are now. Dad would occasionally come home with football boots.

Because I was predominantly right-footed, the toe in my boot would wear out.

He would repair it for me. There was no logic about going straight out and buying a new pair. That didn't

The family silver: Graham was given the 1975/76 championship medal

even happen at Anfield. That was the only perk I had.

I can never remember him coming home with a shirt that had been worn by one of the stars like a Ron Yeats or a Kevin Keegan.

The first time he ever came home with a jersey was after the 1974 FA Cup Final in which Liverpool convincingly beat Newcastle.

He had one of the original shirts, but only because they had bought short sleeved and long sleeved versions for Wembley. Dad was not a great collector of memorabilia. He was never one for having his medals on show.

When he got his first three League Championship medals as a manager, he gave one each to Rob, Christine and myself.

His attitude summed up his modest nature.

There are the famous stories of him putting a box of Championship medals in the Anfield dressing room after another title win and saying 'Take one, but only if you deserve it'.

That was his mentality. He was always looking forward and moving on.

> 'I WOULD GET RIBBED ABOUT BEING BOB PAISLEY'S SON. THE LADS WOULD JOKE THAT I SHOULD BE ABLE TO PLAY BETTER BUT MANY OF THEM WERE PASSIONATE LIVERPUDLIANS AND I ENJOYED MY FOOTBALL AT THAT LEVEL'

'Take one if you deserve it': Medals at Liverpool had to be earned

> to help them individually and to give them every chance. Some may have taken that as a sign of weakness in me. Now the time has come to act to show that I can be as strong as anyone."

What it takes to win the cup – by Paisley

By Alex Goodman, January 24, 1975

What kind of team will win the cup? With his own personal brand of humour, Mr Paisley has the answer to that.

"A team as good as Clemence, Smith, Lindsay, Thompson, Cormack, Hughes, Keegan, Hall, Heighway, Toshack, Callaghan."

And if the significance of that line-up has escaped you, it's the one that triumphed at Wembley last May!

Paisley takes off the gloves

From cutting February 15, 1975

Paisley takes off the gloves

15 FEB 1975

LIVERPOOL boss Bob Paisley took the gloves off in yesterday's talk-in with the Liverpool players following the disappointments of the reverse at Newcastle on Wednesday.

He let them see that when it was a question of discipline he was no shrinking violet, writes Horace Yates.

"I may not shout as loudly as some," he said, "and players can sometimes get hoodwinked by this. I never shout the odds on disciplinary matters.

"I have been in charge of discipline for a long time now and the players have known my feelings all along.

"Because you tread a little softly, some may think it is all easy going.

"I am realistic about football. I realise there has been a change in the modern outlook, but Liverpool are renowned for one thing and that is here. That will not die spirit. That is what some people may have been unwittingly thinking— that nobody is watching away from home.

"When we play as a team we have the best team of all, but only when we play as a team. Never mind the brilliant individuals. They rely on other people working. What I want is the same camaraderie we get at Anfield.

"Liverpool have never been an easy touch and they will never be in the future. Wednesday night was the night for mistakes. It was the same type of night as that at Ajax. You do get this type of game, not that I am prepared to accept it, not that talking is going to do everything.

After a defeat at Newcastle in his first season, Paisley laid down the law to his under-achieving players again:

"I may not shout as loudly as some, and players can sometimes get hoodwinked by this. I never shout the odds on disciplinary matters.

"I have been in charge of discipline for a long time now and the players have known my feelings all along.

"Because you tread a little softly, some may think it is all easy going.

"I am realistic about football. I realise there has been a change in the modern outlook, but Liverpool are renowned for one thing and this is spirit. That will not die here. That is what some people may have been unwittingly thinking – that nobody is watching away from home.

"When we play as a team we have the best team of all, but only when we play as a team. Never mind the brilliant individuals. They rely on other people working. What I want is the same camaraderie we get at Anfield.

"Liverpool have never been an easy touch and they will never be in the future. Wednesday night was the night for mistakes. It was the same type of night as that at Ajax. You do get this type of game, not that I am prepared to accept it, not that talking is going to do everything."

Paisley's new chapter

By Ken Lawrence
March 11, 1975

Despite the fact that Paisley took over from Bill Shankly at the start of the season, he revealed, yesterday, that Saturday's match with Burnley was the first time he had taken his players out of the mould they have used for so long.

"Our match against Burnley was the first step in a change at Anfield. And I think it is time we did change.

"Earlier in the season, I could not alter the old style of play, because the players would not have accepted it. Perhaps, had the pitches this season not been so heavy, then this new idea might not have evolved.

"Anyway, by Saturday, I felt the time had come to change. The players, I think, have matured in the last few months and they

Travelling Kopites: Graham as a fan with wife Sandie on the coach to Paris for the 1981 European Cup final and (below) a 1982 press conference

He would feel every defeat – and sometimes threaten to quit!

Dad never really brought his football home with him. I looked on myself more as a supporter than the son of a famous manager. We sat with the fans near the Kop end where the players and wives had their seats.

There was no hospitality areas and no players' lounges in those early days. We didn't miss those kind of perks because football was very different then.

It was only towards the end of dad's career that we had tickets to the Directors' Lounge when dad was on the board. I can't ever remember any players coming round to our house in Woolton. As a fan I respected the Ian Callaghan's of this world and later Kenny Dalglish who I was lucky enough to meet.

When dad came home, he would only talk about football if you asked him and pushed him. You might imagine that he was going on about it all the time, but the only time it affected us was when his mood changed linked with results.

He would feel every defeat (although there were not too many) and there were occasions when he would come in and say 'That's my lot!' Most of the time, he kept football away from the family as much as he could. When he became manager, the media interest intensified, but it was mainly the local papers the Liverpool Echo and Daily Post, plus the local reporters from the national press. We didn't have all kinds of satellite channels and the like in those days.

The press would ring him on Sunday afternoons, but it wasn't too intrusive and he knew who he could trust. Now the media side of football management is fierce. They expect you to be available all the time. I don't know how dad would have coped with that.

> 'THE PRESS WOULD RING HIM ON SUNDAY AFTERNOONS, BUT IT WASN'T TOO INTRUSIVE. NOW THE MEDIA SIDE OF FOOTBALL MANAGEMENT IS FIERCE. I DON'T KNOW HOW DAD WOULD HAVE COPED WITH THAT'

played in a very grown-up manner against Burnley.

"Liverpool have never been the team to change tactics, we've always played the one way – total commitment to going forward. But so many times this season, we have found to our cost that this method didn't pay.

"We've always entertained, as often away from home as at Anfield. But we've paid, time and time again, for our basic strategy. Now, as we saw on Saturday, with Kevin Keegan pulled back a little from the front line, the style is changing."

The wafer-thin line

By Horace Yates, Summer 1975

Speaking about his first season in charge, Paisley was in philosophical mood: "What is success? I'll tell you. The margin between success and failure is no greater than the width of a crossbar.

"Everybody said what a great season it had been the one before I took over. We won the Cup at Wembley and finished second in the League.

"Of course, it was a great season. It always is when you win a major trophy, but remember the dirty blob on the crossbar at the Anfield Road end after the Doncaster Rovers third-round tie?

"We were as near as that to going out of the Cup at the first fence – and had that happened we would have had just second place in the League to show for a season's work.

"We work on small margins in football. The dividing line is wafer-thin. Perhaps that's why they say you need a bit of luck to be successful.

"I'll admit, right away, that I am disappointed that we did not have a major trophy to show for our efforts. We were in four and we had a good side, but when you count second place as failure, then standards are becoming fantastically high. We never celebrate second place here."

1975-76

Success at home and abroad

Bob answered his critics in the best way possible, claiming his first major trophy after Liverpool edged out QPR in the race for the league title, by just one point.

There had been little transfer activity prior to the start of the season, with defender Joey Jones the only player to come in (from Wrexham) while Chris Lawler and Phil Boersma would be gone by the end of 1975. However, Paisley began to make his mark on the team, with Ray Kennedy transformed from an ineffective forward into a creative midfielder.

An indifferent start had been banished following a run of 23 games with only one defeat. A run of eight wins and one draw in the last nine games would be enough to clinch the crown, with the final game at relegated Wolves. Needing to beat the Midlands side at Molineux on May 4th to overcome top-of-the-table Rangers, the Reds were 1-0 down at half-time courtesy of a Steve Kindon goal before coming back to win 3-1, Keegan, Toshack and Ray Kennedy the goalscorers. Ironically Paisley's Championship success as a player in 1946-47 had also been confirmed on the final day of the season – at Molineux. The five league defeats the Reds suffered was also a record 'best' for the First Division at the time.

Indeed, it was an historic season at home and abroad, as the UEFA Cup was claimed for a second time, the two games being sandwiched by the Wolves fixture. Having seen off Barcelona in the semi-final, the final first leg at Anfield saw the Reds 2-0 down to Club Brugge at half-time. But Paisley's decision to take off John Toshack and bring on Jimmy Case would prove pivotal. Ray Kennedy, Case and Kevin Keegan struck in a six-minute spell around the hour mark to secure a vital 3-2 win.

ROBERT'S STORY

THEY say there's only one Bob Paisley – but that's not true. Robert is the name that the Liverpool manager gave to his first son. There are numerous early pictures in the Paisley family album of Robert with his Dad and brother Graham. While he was forging a career as a professional at Anfield, behind the scenes Bob clearly took great pride and comfort in his two sons.

Robert junior clearly inherited his father's love of sport and, like his father, has maintained a love of cricket. Indeed, Robert has enjoyed a 30-year association with Sefton Park Cricket Club, operating mainly in the role of Membership Secretary.

In 2007, the club's profile was increased as a result of a season-long Sky TV documentary on the plight of amateur cricket clubs and Robert became club chairman, heading a new committee charged with consolidating the club's finances and building a secure future.

Now and then: Robert at Sefton Park and (above) with Dad in 1949

Case recalled: "It wasn't that Tosh was playing badly, but manager Bob Paisley and the coaches felt something had to be changed, the pattern had to be altered."

The second leg three weeks later on May 19th saw the Reds claim a 1-1 draw thanks to Kevin Keegan's goal 15 minutes in (after Liverpool had gone behind to an early penalty), their second triumph in the competition in four years (and second 'Double' success). Indeed, Keegan also won the Football Writers' Player of the Year, while Bob claimed his first Bell's Manager of the Year crown.

Youngsters' time will come

The Bob Paisley Column October 11, 1975

"There is a happy medium in all things and it is my job to bring these lads in when the time is right. It has always been the policy at Liverpool to bring our youngsters along steadily, and there is a right and wrong time to blood them in the top class.

"If you put a lad in too quickly, the mental strain rather than the physical can put him back for months. Some boys have the right mental attitude more than others.

"So our method is to give them ample time to find their feet in Central League games. Last season, we won the League and used 37 players in all. This season, the team has been changed for every match just to give promising lads from the A team a chance in the reserve side. We will continue to do this."

"The club's supporters who write to me about our young lads should appreciate that they don't watch them in away games. And youngsters have to be judged on what they do away as well as at Anfield.

"That is why the reports on these games from the reserve team coach Roy Evans, are so vital."

❯ Paisley reported to League

From article by Michael Charters, March 11, 1976

Bob Paisley has been reported to the Football League for a comment he made to a referee after a vital game.

The referee concerned is John Homewood, of Sunbury-on-Thames, who was in charge of the Derby County-Liverpool game 12 days ago. He booked Kevin Keegan and Tommy Smith and his general handling of the game received widespread criticism.

I know that Mr Paisley was angry at the treatment Keegan received. He was badly fouled in the first few seconds of the game but Mr Homewood did not take any action against the Derby player involved, Henry Newton.

Early in the game, Keegan was cautioned after he had fouled Charlie George. Millions of TV viewers saw George's violent reaction but only Keegan was booked.

After the game, which was drawn 1-1, Mr Paisley made a comment to the referee in the corridor leading to the dressing rooms. Mr Homewood reported this to the League.

I understand that Derby manager Dave Mackay was also disturbed at Mr Homewood's handling of the game. But neither manager would make any public comment – a wise precaution in view of the sensitivity of the League on referees.

Football's top boss – that's Paisley!

Liverpool Echo, May 14, 1976

Liverpool chief Bob Paisley was today acclaimed Manager of the Year for 1976 – a magnificent achievement at the end of only his second season in the Anfield hotseat.

Southampton manager Lawrie ❯

The new Bob Paisley: With Dad again (above) and with the toy car (right) that was a popular Christmas present

Christmas 1987: Only after retiring from the manager's job could Dad spend more time with the family

A toy car and our Christmas dinners after Dad's training

We managed to get married a month after Dad became manager. We had to change the wedding from a Saturday to a Friday because Liverpool were playing a match. We got married in St. Peter's, our local church.

Dad didn't come along and watch us play football at school but in those days not many fathers did.

You'd have the teacher and one parent on the touchline back in those days. Occasionally he would come and look over the wall and say to me afterwards 'you did that right'.

I remember once Mum and Dad bought a toy car and I would drive it in the garden. That was a Christmas present.

We'd have our Christmas meals every year at one o'clock because Dad had always been out training in the morning.

The Paisley Years
IN HEADLINES

McMenemy was mentioned briefly after his team's FA Cup triumph but Mr Paisley's lead in the voting was such that no-one could catch him.

Mr Raymond Miqual, managing director of Bells, presented Mr Paisley with a £1,000 cheque. The trophy will be presented on the Anfield pitch at the first home game next season.

Foreigners wouldn't stand the pace

**Liverpool Echo
May 19, 1976**

Journalist Michael Charters reports a discussion between Paisley and other top football personalities during the Manager of the Year celebrations in Glasgow. At the time Common Market changes looked set to permit a 'free interchange of personnel.'

"The thought of playing 42 League games, and Cup ties, in our long season, on pitches ranging from rock-hard through mud to ice and snow, would frighten them" said Paisley.

"If we did get any foreigners, they'd be the workhorses, the ordinary players. There's no shortage of home-bred players who can do that sort of job for you. But the foreign stars, the people who draw the crowds, wouldn't be interested in coming here.

"It wouldn't be a question of money. Perhaps some club might be prepared to pay the big names the money they want. But would the big names want to play week in, week out, in the demanding English game? They wouldn't find any places to hide.

"On the Continent, the stars only play really tough games now and again. Apart from an elite few teams in each country, the rest of the opposition is poor, so the personality players can take it easy from time to time.

"There are no easy games in England, and I don't think foreigners would stand the pace. In three years or less, they would all go back home."

(These points were heartily agreed on by a circle that included Tommy Docherty, Dave Sexton, Jack Charlton and Gordon Milne)

"There's nothing wrong with the rules. They would be better spending some money and time on better pitches. That would improve the quality of English football immediately," added Paisley.

(At the time there was talk of introducing new ideas, like points for goals)

Paisley responded: "If you can counter opponents' strengths, then you're on the right lines. If you tell one of your own players to do a certain thing, and he goes out there, does it and it works, then his own game is lifted right away. He must think the manager knows what he's talking about!

"But you only instruct defenders and midfield men basically about the opposition. I'd never tell a player like Kevin Keegan what to do. I rely on him to murder the opposition by his own skills. Let them do the worrying and the tactical thinking.

"Watching teams can pay off. In our UEFA Cup run this season, Ray Clemence has saved vital penalties against Hibs and Dynamo Dresden. Each time, he had been told that their penalty takers hit the ball to the keeper's right hand...Ray dived right each time.

"But the Europeans are way ahead of us in one direction. They're up to all the dodges, all the tricks. They know we send men to watch them, that we don't know their players by sight and that we assess them on their

BOYS' PHOTO ALBUM

With Robert at Butlin's in the summer of 1950 – just a couple of months after being left out of the FA Cup final against Arsenal

The Paisley family photo albums

numbers. So they change the numbers around when we play them, trying to confuse us.

"That's happened a few times with Liverpool, and in one match, against Red Star Belgrade I think it was, we changed our numbers around to upset them."

1976-77

Champions of Europe for the first time

Summer changes in the game saw goal average replaced by goal difference in an attempt to encourage goals, while red and yellow cards were introduced for the first time in domestic English football. Changes at Anfield saw David Johnson come in, with Brian Hall and Peter Cormack moving on.

Liverpool came close to completing a historic treble, although Paisley's legacy would be assured courtesy of the club's first European Cup triumph. At that point it was Liverpool's best-ever season.

The League Championship was retained, with the Reds holding Manchester City off by just a point (although the title had been secured in the penultimate game at home to West Ham United, a 0-0 draw), with an unbeaten home record and 18 wins out of 21 at Anfield proving decisive. It was the first time Liverpool had won the league with an unbeaten home record.

With the Reds through to a first European Cup final (having seen off Crusaders, Trabzonspor, St Etienne and FC Zurich), treble dreams remained alive until four days before the showpiece occasion in Italy, when Manchester United claimed a 2-1 victory in the FA Cup final courtesy of a deflected winner past Ray Clemence.

However, that disappointment was made up for on a memorable night in Rome, which saw the Reds triumph 3-1 over West German champions Borussia Moenchengladbach, Terry McDermott, Tommy Smith and

> Phil Neal's penalty sealing matters. May 1977 would also see another major happening in the history of Liverpool Football Club, as a young defender by the name of Alan Hansen moved south of the border from Partick Thistle.

Overall, skipper Emlyn Hughes and Ray Clemence played in every game – 62 in all, including the FA Charity Shield curtain-raiser, which had resulted in a 1-0 victory over Southampton. Kevin Keegan finished with 20 goals in all competitions in what would prove to be his final season with the Reds. Paisley also claimed the Bell's Manager of the Year award, and an O.B.E.

Anfield bosses' Christmas gift

Liverpool Echo, December 22, 1976

A press conference at Anfield revealed the following:

• New seven-year contracts to Paisley and secretary Peter Robinson, starting from New Year's Day.
• The club is to launch into commercialisation in a big way, starting with sponsorship of matches.
• The club's souvenirs, etc. are to be sold worldwide.
• An executive lounge is to be built at Anfield, on the same level as the boardroom, for the matchday use of shareholders.
• The club is to give a lead to Merseyside business and commerce in connection with the Duke of Edinburgh award scheme.

Life's a beach: Relaxing on Newquay beach in Cornwall in June, 1953

Below left: On the beach at Aberystwyth in 1953. Right: At Dalton-le-Dale in 1951

Mr Paisley said: "I would have been perfectly happy to work on a week-to-week basis, for I have never believed in getting anything for nothing, and I don't want anything for nothing out of this. My aim is to fulfil my obligation and if the time ever came when I felt I was not doing that, I would pack in.

"There is no way that I will ever be complacent or take anything for granted.

"I was on a two-year contract and that would have run out in May. I am a realist in this job.

"I know that a lot of good managers have been finished too early.

"That's the way with football and when you come into it you understand the dangers.

"It was not always the same sort of big business that it is today. It's cut throat now.

"I will be the first to know when I have had enough."

Let the pros help to develop youngsters

From newspaper article, February 12, 1977

(This interview was published in the wake of England's 2-0 friendly defeat to Holland at Wembley three days previous)

"I don't pretend to know the answer to the game's problems, but I think there are certain areas which can stand examination and change. But no one can wave a magic wand and sort it all out with some stroke of genius.

"But I do believe the level of football in this country could be improved if we, the professionals in the game, were permitted to give more help to schools and the teachers to encourage promising boy footballers to develop along the right lines.

"In my view, teachers do a great job with the time and facilities at their disposal.

"It is because of these limits that I believe the professionals should be allowed to help them.

"If a boy of eight shows

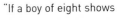

promise he should be allowed to get special tuition and help. That could only come from professional clubs because the teachers are fully occupied in teaching their own subjects, not football.

But at present, clubs are not allowed to take a boy on associated schoolboy forms until he is in his fourth year of secondary education, that is at 14.

We could take a lesson from the continent in this respect. I don't ever want us to follow the way the Communist countries work in sport but it is an eye-opener to see their methods. For example, when Tom Saunders was in Budapest checking on Ferencvaros, he found they ran 22 teams from eight years old upwards.

Paisley: Anfield Iron Man to Indian chief

From Liverpool Echo, May 19, 1977

With a potential haul of League, FA Cup and European Cup on the cards, there had been talk in the press of a treble.

Paisley, in his usual style, was quick to keep everybody's feet on the ground.

He said: "It's all right, the treble, when you say it quickly. Then you realise. You look at the fixtures. Who you've got to play. TWO Cup finals. That, in itself, is frightening.

"Maybe it will be an impossibility. The pressure is going to come now that we are near to it.

"If we beat Manchester United, I'll talk about winning the treble. Only when I've got two. Let's face it.

"Wembley itself is the place where people can freeze on the day. Wembley's not just an ordinary field.

"When you go out there your hair stands on end and that. There's a special atmosphere about it."

On an unnamed summer holiday in 1952. Below: Brotherly fun

Standing with Robert in the fountain at Butlins, 1950

The article concluded in colourful style: 'Paisley folds his arms and leans back in his chair. He has a seamed face, black hair plastered back on his scalp, and looks for all the world like Sitting Bull or some other great Red Indian chief about to lead his braves into battle.'

Over to Healey

From cutting, June 4, 1977

Bob Paisley, named Manager of the Year for the second year in succession...in a contest in which there was not a runner-up in sight, received a cheque for £2,500 as well as a trophy, plus £200 for successes in month competitions.

Commenting on the fact that the prize had been increased from £1,000, Mr Paisley said: "They must have known I was a bit hard up."

On a more serious note, he said it was his opinion that players who left this country should not be allowed to play for England. He said he was not being spiteful, or vindictive, but believed that possibly, if players were denied this opportunity, it might help to keep players in this country.

"I am the first manager in this decade to lose a star player to the continent. The money is not important to me. My interest is building the best team for Liverpool. But, I would be the last to withhold rewards from Keegan.

"Perhaps Denis Healey could help us by easing the tax burden. Somewhere, something has got to be done, otherwise you can't blame anybody for going."

Mr John Smith, the club chairman, said: "This record fee for Keegan is another first for Liverpool, but with our taxation system it is driving people away and providing an inducement for them to go abroad.

"This does not just apply to football, but to other walks of life. We should be able to keep more money in our pay packets.

"This has what has created a brain-drain."

Referring to his managerial award, Mr Paisley said: "I will not fail in any bid for winning this title three years in succession for want of trying. I am tremendously proud, but it all reflects back on the team.

"There was no way I wanted to lose Kevin Keegan, but no club in England could give him the sort of money he is getting in Germany. He has been a tremendous asset to us.

"Life without him will be difficult, for Keegans don't grow on trees – and I have no idea where I can go to get a special replacement for him, but I have to forget about him now."

Deserved recognition for Anfield pair

**Liverpool Echo
June 11, 1977**

The Honours List awards of the O.B.E. to Liverpool manager Bob Paisley and the M.B.E. to Tommy Smith are the Royal acclaim to Liverpool's greatest season, a year of unbelievable achievement and merit.

League champions twice, runners-up once, FA Cup finalists, European Cup winners, UEFA Cup winners.

No other manager in the game has packed such success into the first three years of management.

The award will delight all in football. They will congratulate this modest man, who praises his players and back-room staff without referring to his own mammoth contribution to the Anfield glory days.

A boiling hot day at Newquay, 1953 – Robert wearing the shades!

I would have thought his success could have brought an even higher honour. Sir Matt Busby was knighted after Manchester United triumphed in Europe nine years ago, although he had been manager for 20 years and had become a national figure on a high level.

But Jock Stein received the C.B.E. after Celtic won the European Cup ten years ago.

But national recognition of Liverpool's achievements is the big factor, as Liverpool chairman John Smith told me. He said: "Everyone at the club is delighted at the awards for two men who have spent their working lives at Anfield.

"The directors feel it is recognition of our success over this magnificent season. It is like an award for the club, and I'm sure Bob will regard it in this way, knowing him.

"He has given wonderful service to the game since he joined us before the war...a dedicated, devoted man who lives for football and loves Liverpool.

"The awards also mark another first for Liverpool. I cannot think of any other club who have a manager with the O.B.E., his immediate predecessor also with an O.B.E. and two players each with an M.B.E.

"It is a measure of the high esteem with which Liverpool is regarded throughout the game. We all say, 'well done' to both Bob and Tommy."

Remarkable record of success

Liverpool Daily Post, August 20, 1977

Mr Bob Paisley is now the second longest serving Liverpool employee, having joined them in 1939.

The longest is head groundsman Arthur Riley, 65 this week, who joined the Anfield staff in 1927 and succeeded his father Bert in charge of the Anfield pitch more than 25 years ago.

Jack of all
TRADES

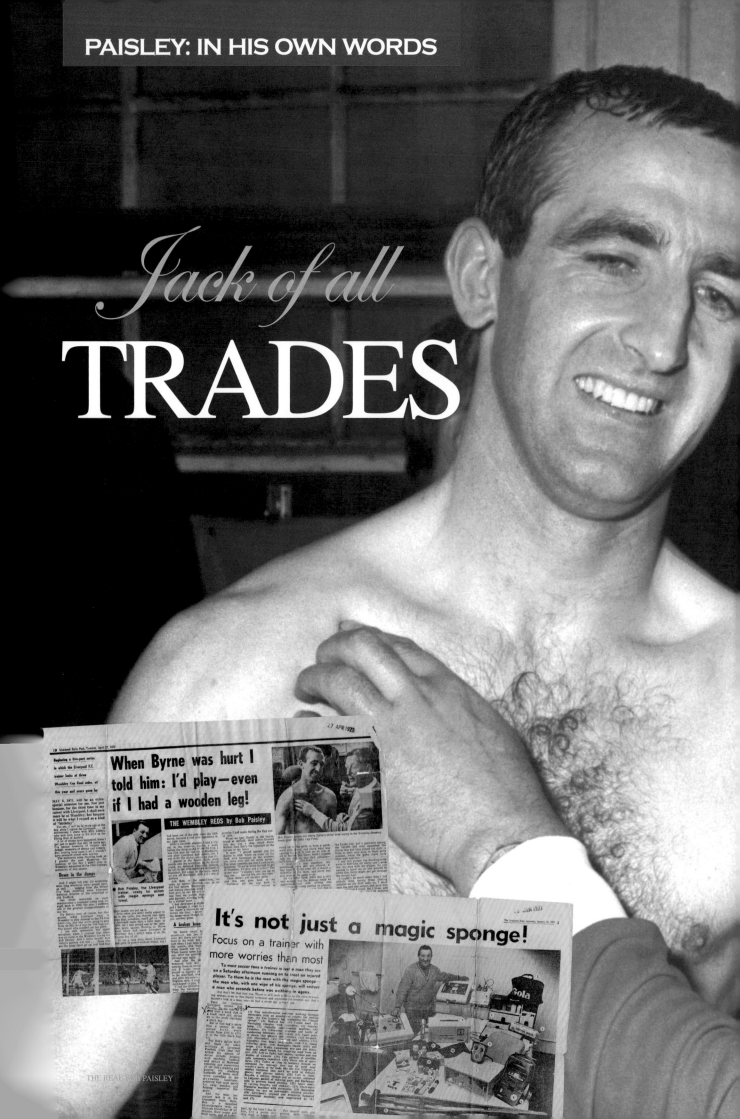

When Byrne was hurt I told him: I'd play — even if I had a wooden leg!

THE WEMBLEY REDS by Bob Paisley

It's not just a magic sponge!

Focus on a trainer with more worries than most

TRAINER. PHYSIO. RESERVE COACH. ASSISTANT MANAGER. PAISLEY FILLED ALMOST EVERY ROLE AT ANFIELD ON HIS WAY TO THE HOTSEAT

1954-1974

Learning the trade

No-one could say that Paisley wasn't qualified for management when he got the Liverpool job in 1974. The Liverpool Daily Post & Echo put the spotlight on the Reds' trainer as he celebrated 30 years at Anfield in 1969. The series of interviews – and others from this time – paint the picture of an eager apprentice learning priceless lessons from Shankly the master

Trainer must play the mind game

**Liverpool Echo,
May 24, 1969**

A trainer's life is one of the busiest of all the jobs associated with running a football club. It is a seven-day-a-week affair. I have to go back a long, long time since I last remember a day during which I didn't set foot in Anfield – and that includes Sundays.

A trainer is a combination of everything. He has to have expert medical knowledge, immense football experience, be quick and alert in summing up any conceivable situation both on and off the field, and when it comes to an injury he must, into the bargain, be something of a psychologist.

You have to know your players inside out. Some need encouragement, others need bullying; and you've got to know which are which, otherwise the

Hauled off by the guards – for having the cheek to try and bring on a sub!

**Liverpool Echo,
May 23, 1969**

Liverpool won a friendly game 2-1 against Real Mallorca at Palmas last night – but civil guards forcibly escorted the Anfield club's trainer Mr Bob Paisley to the dressing room before the game ended.

The incident happened in the 30th minute of the second half after Real had substituted ten of their first half selection.

Mr Paisley stood up in the trainer's box intending to substitute Phil Boersma for Hall and was signalled to sit down by a Majorcan official. He was eventually dragged by two guards to the dressing room.

Paisley said after the match: "I was put in our dressing room and told not to leave. There was nothing else to do but get dressed."

results can be disastrous.

And with injuries too, it's no good telling a player he's going to be off for six weeks, because he becomes lax in his personal life. If he thinks he won't be playing for a few weeks he might be tempted to stay out late, drinking and smoking. And a few days like that can destroy all the work that has been done in his training for months. In many ways you have to be a con man, his injury is only minor and that he could be playing the next Saturday. It's not so different from faith healing for if a player thinks his injury is minor it often happens that it heals quicker.

You must learn to bend the rules

You are acting as the team's 12th man. For despite all the rules that say it's illegal, most trainers are coaching, or passing on advice when they are out there treating injuries.

How many times have you seen a player go down for no apparent reason when his team is under pressure? It's only because he has seen a signal from the bench that the trainer wants to pass on some hints. It's become part of the game but you have to be careful how you do it. You need to use your discretion or else you soon get in trouble with the authorities.

Having a quiet word with the referee

Some (referees) are scared stiff and although it sounds a little like cheating, you sometimes play on this fear.

If the referee hasn't got the personality to stamp his authority on the game, you can exploit that too. And there's been more than one match in which what I've said in passing to a referee while I've been on the pitch has had some influence on how he's controlled the game.

For instance, if I see a player who is unable to beat one of our men fairly and resorts to underhanded tactics, I'll probably draw the referee's attention to it.

All in a day's work: Removing a pitch invader and (opposite) with Peter Thompson

Horses for courses according to ground

It's no good training a team to be world-class sprinters if they've got to operate on heavy grounds. That's when they need the stamina training.

And the work we do at Melwood changes according to what time of winter it is and the conditions that the lads will be operating under."

You have to be a jack-of-all-trades – and a master of them all.

Training to avoid injuries

We have been called a team of supermen; a team that never gets any injuries. This is not luck – just judgement. Dependent on ground conditions likely to be encountered at any particular time so we adjust our training programme.

And our methods of coaching are designed to avoid the player going into tackles that produce injury. He is taught to tackle in such a fashion that is equally effective but minimises the risk.

And it is the boss, Bill Shankly who must take the credit for evolving this system and surely its success has been proved by the number of ever-presents, or almost so, that we have every season. Last year for instance, five were ever-present, and nine of the team played in 38 or more matches.

Keeping an eye on the dressing room superstitions

One of the oldest and most common is being last out. And it's a real battle at Anfield between Emlyn Hughes and Ian St John. Both like to be last and there's usually a jostling session in the doorway before they agree to run out together.

Billy Liddell was like that too, but then he was made captain and had to be first out!

Tommy Smith and Ian Callaghan have a ritual where, no matter how loose their jerseys are already, they both tug each other's and stretch ▶

What is a trainer?

On the bench you're the team's 12th man. Despite the rules, most trainers are coaching when they are out there treating injuries.

As told to CHRIS JAMES

Cup final advice a life and death affair

Liverpool Daily Post
April 27, 1971

My mind goes back to the 1965 final, quite early on in the game, when I went on the field to attend to an injury which our left-back, Gerry Byrne, had received. He and Leeds United inside-forward Bobby Collins had collided and Gerry had quite a gash down a shin. It was painful, of course, but it looked worse than it was. I was soon satisfied that it wouldn't cause Gerry to quit.

I was far from satisfied a few minutes later, though, when I saw Gerry taking a throw-in. For as he was about to throw the ball, I noticed him wince, as if something was really giving him trouble.

The next time play was stopped, I raced on to the pitch to check what was causing the pain. It took me no time at all to realise that Gerry hadn't injured only his shin in

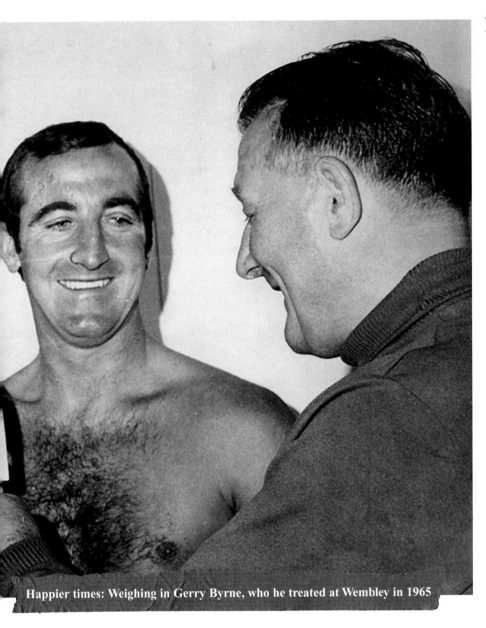

Happier times: Weighing in Gerry Byrne, who he treated at Wembley in 1965

them before they put them on. And it has to be those two involved in the ritual. No-one else will do.

Peter Thompson will always make two or three trips to the treatment table before a match while Ron Yeats and St John are the dressing room jokers, laughing and shouting.

Tommy Lawrence and Chris Lawler, both have such placid temperaments that they just get changed but I'm sure, that whatever kit I laid out, they'd put it on – even if I substituted Wellington boots for their football boots.

Ian Callaghan, always like to be first at the ground and it's a long time since anyone beat him to it.

Kopites shouldn't clap opposition keepers!

There cannot be a more fair-minded crowd than there is at Anfield. If a team is doing well, they are appreciated, and the players love it. What does upset the lads, however, is the obscenities a few hot-heads shout from the terraces.

Like everyone else at Anfield, they're proud of the name 'Liverpool' and they don't like anything that makes a smear against that name.

There's one thing they've got that few crowds have these days – sportsmanship.

But I think they take it a bit far sometimes. Every week they give a massive cheer to the visiting goalkeeper and invariably this is the spur for him to have a blinder.

Injury hunch that helped us to promotion

We lost 1-0 at Rotherham and it was at Millmoor that Ron Yeats fell badly and injured his scaphoid – a small bone in the wrist.

In my playing days I'd had a similar injury and I remember it was terribly painful. He went for an x-ray which showed a fracture and they put his wrist in plaster.

When we went back to have the plaster off, I asked Ron if his hand hurt – it was to prove a chance

that first collision – he'd broken his collar bone. I was in a real quandary, for substitutes were still not allowed at that time. If Gerry came off, it meant a reshuffle of the team and there was still most of the game to go. On the other hand, there was a very real danger that the damage could be aggravated – and with serious consequences – if Gerry carried on playing. I had no option but to warn him that if he took another blow, or even if the ball should catch him heavily, the break could be reversed and the bone could turn inwards and puncture a lung.

Gerry realised that one man could make the decision – himself. He looked at me for help, though and asked: "What would you do, Bob?" In a flash, I realised that I couldn't tell this fellow to quit the field. I

had a vision of 1950 and the terrible feeling I had had, when I realised I wouldn't be treading that famous turf. Something deep inside me made me answer: "If it was me I would play – even if I had a wooden leg."

Gerry nodded and I thought I could see the relief in his eyes, despite the pain he would have to endure. I put a horseshoe pad on that damaged shoulder, gave hurried instructions to Willie Stevenson to keep a close watch on him and returned to my touchline seat, wondering if I had said the right thing.

I was on tenterhooks and ready to spring from my seat every time the ball went near Gerry. But he was still there at the end . . . and when he walked up to the royal box to collect his winner's medal no one knew what it had cost him in effort and agony.

remark that may well have won Liverpool promotion. For although the wrist has little to do with football, a scaphoid fracture is, as I say, extremely painful and Ron would have been out for some time.

And he was already immensely valuable to the team and I wouldn't like to say what would have happened without him.

When he answered, he said: 'It's only a slight pain Bob.'

Now this surprised me for I remembered that when they had taken my plaster off, I almost went through the roof with the pain. And then Ron mentioned that he had received a similar injury before.

Having had the injury before it all clicked into place and I suspected that the old injury had never healed properly and that, in fact, he had not broken it this time – it was just that the bones had never knitted together again from the previous injury.

We went up to Dundee and toured the hospitals until we found the one with the old x-ray plates from his former injury.

And all the plates, even those after the plaster was off, showed there was still a break – confirming what I had thought.

So it wasn't as bad a blow as it had first seemed and Ron was able to play the rest of the season with his wrist in a leather strap. And with Ron in the side we galloped to promotion.

Learning to be as ruthless as Shanks

After Watford (FA Cup defeat in 1970), manager Bill Shankly was in thoughtful mood, as we made the journey home. So was I. So were many people in the party.

Loyalty cuts two ways. The players who had gone on and on had done magnificently for Liverpool over the years; and they had earned every word of praise which had been bestowed upon them. And yet – the manager and his staff owed it to the club and the supporters to make sure that there was no slide downhill to oblivion.

The show must go on despite secret cartilage agony

A helping hand for the injured Emlyn Hughes

Liverpool Daily Post, May 14, 1971

Fate's final cruel twist of the season came yesterday when Liverpool's trainer, Bob Paisley, was confirmed as another cartilage victim – the fourth of the season at Anfield.

He goes into hospital on Tuesday and will have his operation on Thursday, so that he has to stand down from the club's Scandinavian tour. This will be his second operation for cartilage trouble. The first, about three years ago, was on his left knee. This time the trouble lies with the right.

The breakdown came the day before (the 1971 FA Cup final which Liverpool lost to Arsenal) at Wembley. The cartilage slipped out during a five-a-side game but Bob retired for a few minutes, slipped the cartilage back in position, tightly bound the knee and carried on.

Nobody was aware of the breakdown and he was able to complete his duties at Wembley.

'THE CARTILAGE SLIPPED OUT DURING A FIVE-A-SIDE GAME BUT BOB RETIRED FOR A FEW MINUTES, SLIPPED THE CARTILAGE BACK IN POSITION, TIGHTLY BOUND THE KNEE AND CARRIED ON ... NOBODY WAS AWARE OF THE BREAKDOWN'

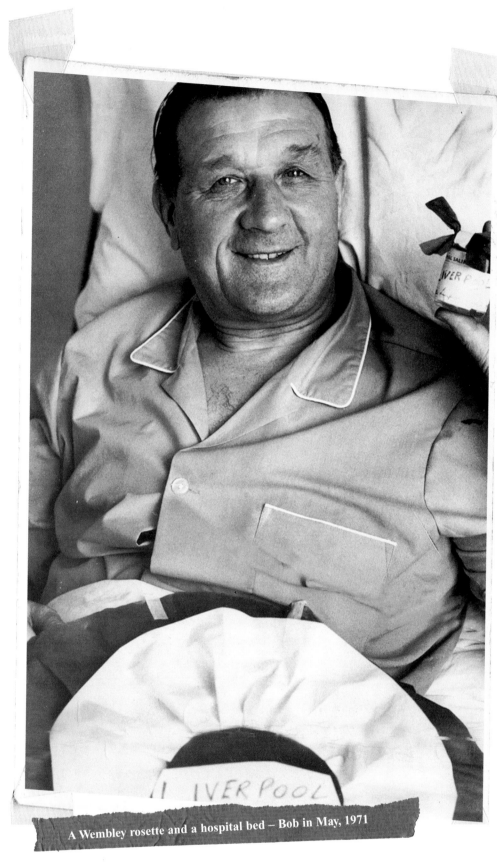

A Wembley rosette and a hospital bed – Bob in May, 1971

The decision was taken: changes must be made. If Bill Shankly was plagued by gnawing doubts, no one was ever allowed to see it. But he did not hide the fact that it came hard, to break up a team such as Liverpool had had.

Typically, once the decision had been made, Bill plunged into the task. And as he had done when he fashioned the great side of the 60s, he went straight down the middle.

Ray Clemence took over in goal, and Larry Lloyd, a £50,000 recruit from Bristol City, went in at No. 5.

Steak a day on my advice for young star

At the start of the 1970/71 season, Bill made a big decision – to plunge young John McLaughlin into First Division football.

The lad was tremendously skilful, had a fine footballing brain; but the question was whether his stamina would last 90 gruelling minutes.

The boss really wanted to blood John gently but events forced us to pile on the pressure. These past few weeks John has been out of the team...but he's a long way from being out of Bill Shankly's plans for the future.

Almost a year ago, as the boss and I were discussing John's potential and the wisdom of throwing him in at the deep end, we were deliberating how to build him up, physically.

I suggested that steak might be a good thing.

Bill mused and mused and when we parted I could tell that he was still thinking things over.

On the Monday morning when I walked into Anfield I was greeted with the news that the boss had ordered a steak every day for John McLaughlin – right through the summer.

There aren't many who can claim to be Liverpool Lifers – men who have devoted a lifetime's service to Liverpool Football Club but Paisley was certainly one of them. Perhaps none, though, can boast such a wide and varied Anfield CV. His first three seasons as manager had seen a massive improvement as Paisley transformed his team from also-rans to Treble challengers. Once he had reached the summit of European football, he was in no mood to climb down.

Bob in arsenal

...standing, he never left the field and

Billy Liddell

1933, Bob in his Durham County cap

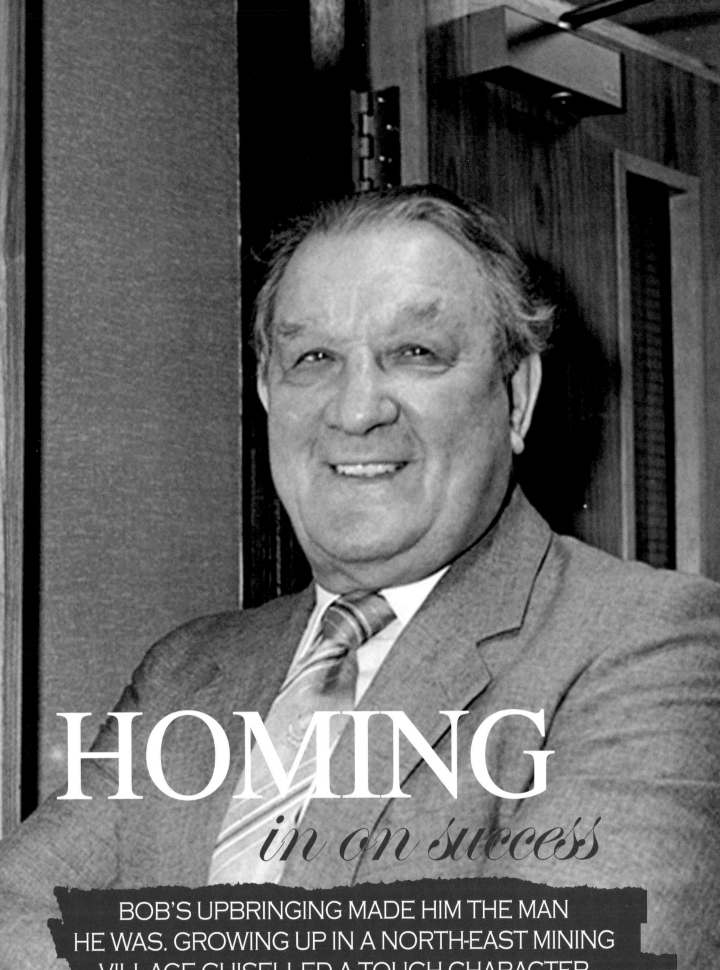

HOMING
in on success

BOB'S UPBRINGING MADE HIM THE MAN
HE WAS. GROWING UP IN A NORTH-EAST MINING
VILLAGE CHISELLED A TOUGH CHARACTER
DETERMINED TO SUCCEED IN LIFE

> Bob Paisley started the 1977-78
season as manager of the
European champions and in
charge of the team that everyone
wanted to beat in the First
Division. But a major star had
departed the Anfield stage in the
form of Kevin Keegan. Time
would only tell how the Reds
would adapt to life without their
dynamic number 7. Paisley
broke the bank to bring in a
replacement for Keegan, paying
£440,000 to buy Kenny Dalglish
from Celtic.

1977-78

King Kenny inspires
Double champions

Paisley was forced to make a
major change to his side prior to
the new season following the sale
of Kevin Keegan to West German
Bundesliga side Hamburg in a
£500,000 deal. To replace him
would be a player who had
already plundered a century of
goals in Scottish football, Celtic's
Kenny Dalglish who cost a British
record fee. He would prove an
ideal replacement.

Other changes to Liverpool
personnel included the £352,000
signing of Graeme Souness from
Middlesbrough – a record fee
between English clubs at that
stage. Amongst those out of the
Anfield exit door were Alan
Waddle, Alec Lindsay and John
Toshack mid-season, on a free to
Swansea City where he would
take over as player-manager and
guide the Welsh side from Fourth
to the First Division in
consecutive seasons.

Unfortunately, Dalglish's
contribution (he would score 31
goals in all competitions, playing
all 62 games that season) would
not be enough to secure a hat-
trick of titles, the Reds finishing
as runners-up. Brian Clough's
Nottingham Forest took the top
flight by storm following their
promotion, taking the title by
seven points and also securing
the League Cup – Liverpool
falling 1-0 in a replay.

HUGHIE'S STORY

Speaking to Hughie Paisley, the only real reminder of his illustrious older brother is the accent. Until he gets out of his armchair, that is. He eases into his coat, picks up his walking stick and adjusts his flat cap. Then the resemblance becomes strikingly obvious.

Hughie is 85 and the surviving Paisley brother is not in the best of health after suffering a stroke. However, the opportunity to go out round Hetton and re-visit the places that shaped Bob's life was one he was delighted to undertake.

There can be no prouder brother than Hughie, who lives close to Hetton town centre. He gets very emotional when talking about "Our Bob". More than once during an extended conversation about their shared upbringing, he became choked up as he recalled the achievements of the town's most famous son.

The main thoroughfare in Hetton is Front Street and the Paisley family had a tiny house there when Bob was born in January 1919. It was at number two Office Place, where there was a row of three houses. Eldest brother Bill and Bob were born while they lived there and with only one room upstairs and one down, parents Samuel and Emily soon had to find somewhere bigger. A community centre and car park now stand on the site.

The family moved to a rented house on 'The Avenue', where they lived when Hughie and youngest brother Alan came into the world. Samuel was working down the mines and eventually he was given the chance of a colliery house, rent-free, on Nicholas Street in 1925. Hughie was three at the time and Bob six. When Alan came into the world another room was required so they moved again three years later, on this occasion to 31 Downs Lane. It had two bedrooms, a room downstairs and a kitchen. From his earliest memories, Hughie recalls that Bob was always kicking a ball about. That's all his mind focused on.

School days: A rare early picture of Bob

The soup kitchen – and the day Dad pulled Bob out of the pit

Memories: Hughie outside his house in Hetton in 2005

In 1926, when Bob was seven, the mines were only working two days a week and Dad's wages were meagre.

The whole area suffered as this state of affairs persisted for nine months. It was desperate times and the school or soup kitchen would provide us with one meal a day.

Bob would often take a can to the soup kitchen, fill it, take it home and we would all share out the contents. That's all we had.

Around this time, Bob would join our older brother Willie in pushing a barrowload of coal down the hill in Hetton from Downs Lane to his grandmother's home, which was

about a mile away and close to where I live now, near the Fox and Hounds pub.

For steering the barrow, with its mangled wheels, he got a penny and I got a ha'penny and an apple.

Bob played for the senior Barrington school team when he was in the juniors but it was after transferring to Eppleton at 11 that his football really took off and he never looked back leaving the school three years later with 13 winners' medals.

After leaving school, Bob joined his dad at the pit but my father was badly injured in 1935 so he said to Bob: 'Out of the pit, you'. That very same day, he was out of the pit.

There would be generous consolation in European competition though. A first European Super Cup was secured 7-1 on aggregate against Kevin Keegan's Hamburg, including a 6-0 humiliation for the former Reds hero at Anfield in the second leg.

The European champions would also successfully defend their title. Having been given a bye in round one due to their status as holders, the Reds saw off Dynamo Dresden, Benfica and Borussia Moenchengladbach. The final was a scrappy affair at Wembley Stadium, but the 1-0 victory over Club Brugge of Belgium was all that mattered, with Dalglish the match-winner.

In other competitions, Paisley's men shared the FA Charity Shield with Manchester United after a 0-0 draw, while in the FA Cup Chelsea claimed a 4-2 win in the third round. Phil Neal was the only other player to play all 62 games, with Ray Kennedy (61), Ray Clemence (60) and Emlyn Hughes (59) also prominent.

That's the end of the social whirl

From cutting
By Charles Lambert
September 26, 1977

Paisley let his feelings show in the wake of a 1-0 win over Derby County at Anfield:

"The supporters have killed them with kindness. It is not something physical that you can improve by going for a run round the houses. It is the mental attitude. The first few yards are in your head in this game.

"The players are having too many entertainments. All right, I know they are for good causes, but you just can't go on like this. I'm not saying they are going out boozing, but they are constantly being invited out to places. The European Cup has brought added pressure – it has for me, anyway.

"I'm not being a spoil-sport. I know people expect to see the players, but they also expect them to play well."

Fish and chips off

> ## Bob wins TV praise

**From cutting,
December 29, 1977**

'He's magic. He's smashing.' That is just the supporters'' estimation of Liverpool manager Bob Paisley.

And last night his friends, his team and the greats of the soccer world paid even more touching tributes to Bob on Eamonn Andrews' TV programme This Is Your Life.

They spoke of his quiet dedication, his tenacity, his loyalty and efficiency.

Sir Matt Busby, now on the Manchester United board but Liverpool's captain when Bob

joined the Anfield club, said he had not been surprised when his former team-mate had taken Liverpool to the greatest prize in club football.

Sir Matt added: "He's prepared to give everyone else the limelight rather than himself and this is a very rare thing these days.

"He would always put his club before himself. He has this inner steel to motivate players to great heights."

From Hetton to Paris: 1981 celebrations

When my father was injured, by, we had a rough time. My oldest brother was working at the colliery as well – he was a blacksmith. When he was 20 he got finished because he was going to come into bigger money so they let him go.

I hadn't started work. It was very tough. You had 17 shillings and 6 pence compensation for his arm and we had to pay 7 and 6 rent out of that. Ten shillings had to do us. My mother went down to the parish where we lived and she got a 25 shillings voucher.

Our dad was a big, strong fella. My dad should have been a heavyweight boxer. He was a quiet fella but anybody who ruffled him would suffer. She was a canny woman, my mother. A placid woman.

After his dad forced him to quit the pit, Bob had to look for a new job and got one with a mate, George Oxley, who was an apprentice bricklayer.

It was at Blackhall, 12 mile away. We got an old bike off Uncle Dave, my father's brother, and Bob used to pedal from the Downs Lane to Blackhall, 12 mile and 12 mile back. 24 mile a day – a boy on an old bike.

When he got back to Downs Lane, Bob ate his dinner before going out to meet his mates outside the ice cream shop on Front Street. They'd then walk two miles to the cinema in Houghton. After the show was over, they'd walk back the two miles to Hetton and end the evening with a chip supper from Warlock's fish shop.

The woman who served him would later give birth to a boy called Alan Kennedy. (Sadly, she died before Bob signed her son for Liverpool in 1978).

future star's mum

It started here: Bob's early family home

'BOB USED TO PEDAL FROM DOWNS LANE TO BLACKHALL, 24 MILES A DAY, ON AN OLD BIKE. WHEN HE GOT BACK TO DOWNS LANE, BOB ATE HIS DINNER BEFORE GOING OUT TO MEET HIS MATES OUTSIDE THE ICE CREAM SHOP'

> **Bob Paisley This Is Your Life**

Liverpool Echo, December 29, 1977

The show was recorded in November and Mrs Paisley was first told on August 1.

From that moment, she had the seemingly impossible task of making sure the Paisley home life ran normally, despite the fact that she and the family were involved with Mr Leonard (TV official Maurice Leonard) in working out all the long-forgotten little details which confront the embarrassed celebrity.

Bob told me: "I had no idea that anything was going on.

"There was one or two little things which I realised later were out of the usual, but these were at the club, not at home.

"Jessie kept it the complete secret. I didn't have a clue."

The major keep-it-secret manoeuvres happened on the day of the match (at QPR).

ITV needed a film crew on the team bus and their excuse was that they were from German TV, recording Liverpool before their Super Cup games against Hamburg.

Director Royston Mayor, speaking broken English with an impressive German accent, called himself Herr Dortmunder and got away with it until he lapsed into Irish-English for a moment in all the excitement. But Bob didn't hear it.

While the match was on, the bus parked away from the ground and Eamonn Andrews was smuggled on board dressed in the casual gear of a TV technician.

After the game, players and officials piled onto the coach on the way back to Euston, chairman John Smith directed Bob to sit next to him in a seat nominated as the best for the cameras and the blazing TV lights were switched on.

Bob chatted normally as the camera operator moved up the

coach, apparently filming the players.

But something stirred at the back of the coach, hidden from view before this by the TV crew.

It was the bold Eamonn, stealthily making his way forward to appear before Bob Paisley, timed to the second as the bus stopped near the TV studio. The rest you know...if you saw the programme.

ITV throw money away on this show as though there's no tomorrow.

It cost them £1,000 for the air fare alone to fly Bob's pal Frank Carr from Hong Kong to appear on the show.

Their London hotel bill for that weekend ran into thousands. It was £50 a night for two – without meals.

Jessie Paisley and her family had a hectic, but totally memorable weekend in London. And it was Jessie who told me the real punchline in the whole show, an incident which almost sank it without trace before a camera rolled.

Two months before the programme, Bob went to his old home in County Durham to show his friends the League Championship trophy and the European Cup.

He had a great day, feted by the village dignitaries.

But he told Jessie afterwards that many of his old pals hadn't turned up and he wondered why that was.

Of course, Jessie knew the answer, but could say nothing to Bob.

What he knows now is that the TV people had a near fit when they heard of his trip because he was going to meet people they had ear-marked for the show, with Eamonn chanting...

"And here's your old pal, Charlie what's-it ... whom you haven't seen for 40 years."

Bob was going to see Charlie and others a few weeks earlier until the This Is Your Life crew got busy and made sure they were "missing" when the cups came in.

Winning the Pools made us 'posh' but all that Bob cared about was football

Kop tour: Jessie, Bob and Hughie with wife Mary at Anfield in 1983

I also started work as a bricklayer in Hartlepool in 1936 but I was only making six and fivepence a week.

The family was living from day to day until we happened to have a bit of luck.

The (Littlewoods) Pools was our saviour. I think I got 14 out of 15 teams right.

I had York City to beat Port Vale in an away match and Port Vale beat them 2-1, otherwise we would have had £9,000.

But we were quite happy with the £315, nine shillings and a penny.

We were millionaires! We were real posh. The first thing my father said was 'I'm having a new coat'. I can't think what our Bob wanted.

It's almost certain it would have been something to do with football. That's all he thought about.

That's all his mind was set on.

He never used to bother with girls. Football, football, football.

Nothing else mattered, just the football.

> Bob's record without equal

Liverpool Echo, May 11, 1978

Just think what he could command elsewhere if his loyalties weren't bound so strongly to Anfield.

The rather surly Ernst Happel, the Bruges coach and manager of the Dutch national team, earned £80,000 a year at Bruges, who have never won a European trophy. He gets that incredible salary just for keeping them as the top club in Belgium.

Such a record pales by comparison with the Liverpool manager's successes.

A man very close to Liverpool said to me: "If Bob were mercenary, he could get a £100,000 a year job in Europe just for the asking. His record speaks for itself."

Putting that point to the man himself, he smiled and said: "Not interested."

For that, believe me, everyone associated with Liverpool – official, player and supporter – should be grateful.

Paisley – toast of car workers

Liverpool Echo, May 18, 1978

Thousands of production workers at Vauxhall's Ellesmere Port plant gave a tumultuous welcome to that master of European hustle Bob Paisley.

Bob was attending the latest in a series of lunchtime chats with sporting personalities at the factory laid on by journalist and Tranmere Rovers chairman Bill Bothwell.

Bob was given some straight questions by the workers. Was Kenny Dalglish worth £440,000?

"Kenny has had a tremendous season. The money doesn't come into it. It was the exchange of one great player for another. We couldn't keep Keegan and were

Rejected . . . but

lucky enough to get Dalglish."

Were Liverpool about to sign Derek Johnston from Rangers? "I didn't know he played for Rangers! No, we probably want better players than him."

Will Keegan be back? "There is no way he will come back into English football. He'll go to America or Spain after Germany."

There was a surprise in store for the Liverpool manager. First, he was introduced to Stan Spencer, who served right through the war with him in Egypt and Italy, with the 73rd Medium Artillery.

Stan, the 58-year-old data processing manager at the factory, said: "We haven't met since the war, but I have seen plenty of Bob on television."

Owzat! Bob has the opposition stumped

**Liverpool Echo,
June 5, 1978**

Bob Paisley swapped his tracksuit for the cricketer's flannels at Oxton, Wirral.

And Bob showed he had a touch of class in this game too – he picked up two wickets with his medium pace bowling and made 10 runs with the bat to become his team's second top scorer.

Bob's long shot

**Liverpool Echo
August 11, 1978**

As Liverpool prepared for another demanding season, Paisley was in thoughtful mood.

He told the Echo: "We do most of our shooting from inside the penalty area and do it well.

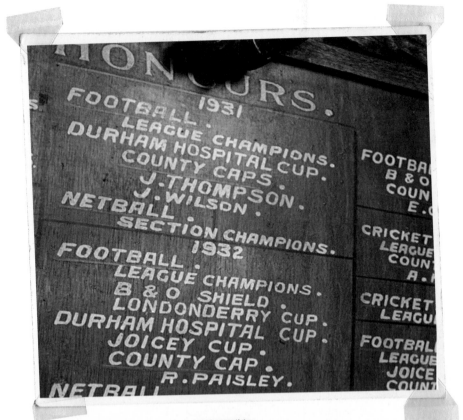

Name in high places: Eppleton School honours board from the early days (above) and Hughie pointing out a plaque at the former home in Hetton

You could see that he was going places. The boys of Hetton would play whenever they could.

They used to say at one time that you just had to shout down the pit shaft and you'd get half a dozen footballers. There was rarely anything else for them to do. Everybody was in to football then.

Not quite everyone though. The local farmer was unhappy if we played near his land. We used to have to go a mile and a half up the side of the pit heaps in a field to play football. We knew it was wrong but it was the only place where you could play. We would just be starting and enjoying ourselves and the farmer would come and take it away.

Bob was rejected by Wolves and

his beloved Sunderland as a teenager. Sunderland had a change of heart when they heard Liverpool wanted to sign him but Bob refused to go back on an agreement to join the Reds.

He went down to Sunderland for a trial and they said: 'Ohhh, you're too small'. Later, Liverpool came up. That was the club he wanted to be at, so when Liverpool came on to the scene and said they would sign him, Sunderland went 'We'll sign you, Bob'. 'No', he says, 'I've made a promise and I never break a promise. I'm going to Liverpool'. You can see Sunderland's loss now, can't you?

When he retired in 1983, (Tom) Cowie, the Sunderland chairman, came down to see Bob and asked him if he would sign for them. Bob said: 'Mr Cowie, you're too far gone'.

a promise is kept

'HE WENT DOWN TO SUNDERLAND
FOR A TRIAL AND THEY SAID:
'OHHH, YOU'RE TOO SMALL'.
LATER, LIVERPOOL CAME UP.
WHEN LIVERPOOL CAME ON TO
THE SCENE, SUNDERLAND WENT
'WE'LL SIGN YOU, BOB'

"But perhaps we do too much of it and we should be ready to shoot from longer range.

"When hit correctly from inside the area, the ball flies true and straight at the keeper. We must now work hard at shooting from further out and producing that last few feet of swerve and fade which we saw so often in Argentina.

"Against Bayern Munich (pre-season friendly) the other night, our shooting let us down. We should have won easily but we were trying to work the ball too close to the keeper before shooting. We must have a go from outside the box.

"We'll be putting more emphasis on this from now on. It's no use encouraging the boys to do it at this stage of training because they would kick their legs off. But as the season gets going, we'll be doing plenty of it at Melwood.

"If we can improve our shooting I think we'll be a match for anyone. We should have another good season."

Talking of the new season's plans, Paisley added: "They are European champions and there's a lot of pride at stake when they go on the field, whatever the opposition. They want to win as well as get fit...and I'm not complaining at that attitude.

"Most of them have been winning honours for years, and they get used to it. So it is not easy to motivate them with words. The motivation for Liverpool players, who have done it all practically, is to have competition for places in the first team. That is the best motivation for all and that's what we've achieved at Anfield.

"We have a strong first team squad of 16 and they all get the same basic wage whether they play or not. But being good professionals, they all want to play in every match. That is what competition for places means; that is what motivates them now.

"I am glad we are going to sign Alan Kennedy from Newcastle. He is a fine young full-back, very good at going forward. He'll provide more challenge in the defence and I've been thinking a good deal about that department recently.

"I think Emlyn Hughes is best used now at centre-back, when he is in his best form. I have moved him there from left-back during this tour because I had the possible incoming of Kennedy in mind.

"We have competition for all back four places now, in midfield, and also up front, where it seems as though David Johnson has made a good recovery from his knee operation. The competition between them all is what I have been trying to achieve.

"We are at our best with four men in midfield. I know some people think this is negative, that we only play with two forwards – Kenny Dalglish with either Steve Heighway or David Fairclough or David Johnson.

"It may look like that, but only on paper. We play with five forwards, because Ray Kennedy, Jimmy Case and Terry McDermott move up constantly to play as attacking forwards. It is nonsense to talk about a two-man forward line."

1978-79

Records broken for free-scoring champs

Bob Paisley's third league success in four seasons and Liverpool's 11th Championship was arguably his most impressive, secured following a 3-0 victory over Aston Villa in May – the 40th anniversary of Paisley's arrival at Anfield.

Strengthened by the signing of Alan Kennedy (out went Tommy Smith, Ian Callaghan and Joey Jones), the champions' winning margin was a massive eight points ahead of runners-up Nottingham Forest (who despite losing only three games compared to the Reds' four, drew 18 games).

They won 30 of their 42 games

Gunner Paisley: Army photos and memorabilia kept by the family

'Desert Rats' and

O ur Bob had never left the north-east when he caught the train to Liverpool in 1939 but within a year he was travelling the world.

He did not choose to. He had been called up to fight for his country in the Second World War.

He served in the 73rd regiment of the Royal Artillery, based in

Tarporley, but was then stationed abroad for more than four years. He joined up with Field Marshall Montgomery's Desert Rats, serving as a driver to a reconnaissance officer for much of the time, fighting his way through North Africa, Sicily and Italy.

Bob thought he got blinded one time. He was in the trenches and a

ROYAL ARTILLERY

an absent brother

plane came over and sprayed them with bullets. His eyes were full of sand and he thought he was blinded.

While we both came home safely from war-time service, youngest brother Alan didn't.

I was about to go abroad when we got word about my youngest brother dying in 1944.

He was only 14 and died of scarlet fever and diptheria. I'll never forget, the Major said 'I'll send word up to your parents that you can't come to the funeral'.

I said 'If you don't give me permission to go to that lad's funeral, I'm away tonight'.

I would, I would have gone. I got fortnight 'jankers' when I got back because I came back two days late.

whilst also conceding only 16 goals, scoring 85 and claiming a record points tally of 68 in the process. Kenny Dalglish's contribution was rewarded by the Football Writers', who awarded him their Player of the Year award. In all Liverpool averaged two goals a game (earning a 'reward' from a national newspaper in the process), with the most memorable match being the 7-0 demolition of Tottenham in September, the seventh, scored by Terry McDermott, inspiring the following quote from Paisley:

"That must be the best goal Anfield has ever seen."

The performance was summed up thus by Michael Charters in Monday's Liverpool Echo (4/9/78):

'Have you ever heard 50,000 people purr with pleasure? Well, the Anfield spectators were doing that constantly as Liverpool stroked the ball around with one-touch moves of staggering accuracy. This display confirmed for me, particularly after the splendour of their wins at Ipswich and City the previous week, that the current Liverpool team is playing better, more exciting, attacking football than any side I've seen since the war.'

Unfortunately there was to be no hat-trick of European Cups, as the holders were beaten in the first round by English champions Nottingham Forest, in the days before seedings were introduced to the competition. There was also disappointment in the European Super Cup, as the Reds lost 4-3 on aggregate to Anderlecht.

In the other cup competitions there was an early exit to Sheffield United in the League Cup, while in the FA Cup Paisley's Double dream was ended with a 1-0 defeat to Manchester United in a semi-final replay at Goodison Park.

Kenny Dalglish, Ray Kennedy and Phil Neal played all 54

games while Graeme Souness and Ray Clemence missed only one game (in the European Super Cup), with King Kenny top-scoring with 25 goals. Paisley also won his third Bell's Manager of the Year honour in four years.

Anniversary Waltz time!

**Liverpool Echo
May 5, 1979**

Talking at the end of another successful campaign, Paisley remarked: "We don't have any secrets about our success. We regard football as a simple game but perhaps what gives us something extra is the spirit in the club.

"We are dedicated to two things – the family and winning. We are a family club, everyone helping everybody else in every department. That is the spirit which runs right through all club policy. We never want to lose; we make a custom of winning.

"For myself, as manager, I have two things – my own family, without which nothing could be achieved. Without that as the basis, no man can succeed. And I have the staff at Anfield, helping me all along the line. Without them, I couldn't achieve anything at Anfield.

"As manager, the pressures are greater now than I've ever known as a player or coach. When you're at the top, the pressure is on you to stay there; if you're in the middle, you're under pressure at the bottom, the pressure to get higher.

"But I wouldn't want to be without pressure. I love to be involved in it and I'm learning all the time.

"In my first year as manager, I made a habit of counting ten before I made a decision. I was cautious – deliberately. I took my bends wide instead of hugging the rails, probably because I was so keen not to trip up.

"Now I'm learning, now I count only two before I make a decision.

Bob: The miner's son who deserved more than he got for his efforts!

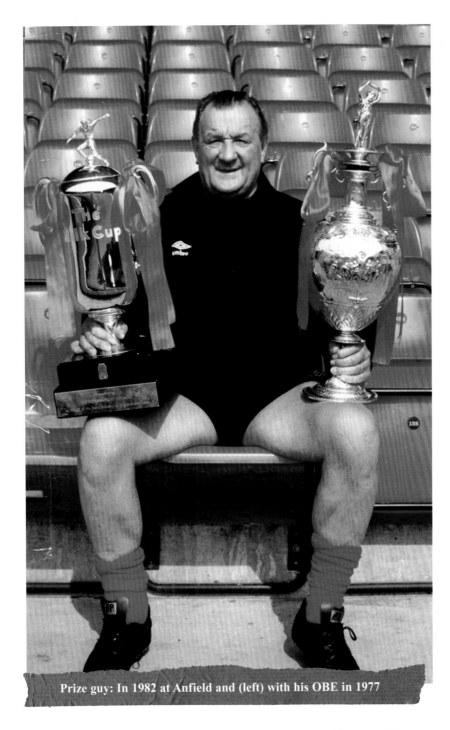

Prize guy: In 1982 at Anfield and (left) with his OBE in 1977

> That's what management teaches you.

"We go along at Liverpool, day by day. We have our patterns and our way of life.

"We set our targets and ambitions at the very top and it's pressure to stay there. But I wouldn't be without it, I wouldn't change a day of it.

"I'm happy, keep good health and am surrounded by good friends and helpers. I've no thoughts of retiring, I'm 60 but I believe I've got a few years left in the job. I hope so anyway because I enjoy my work."

"I've no doubt about the greatest thing that's happened in my 40 years – Rome 1977. I always thought winning the FA Cup for the first time in 1965 was No 1 but Rome beat that.

"That is because everything was so right – the performance of the team, the venue and the atmosphere, the wonderful supporters, it was all unbelievable.

"Winning the European Cup for the first time must be the greatest of all the great times and days I've had with Liverpool."

It's a Paisley treble

From cutting
May 26, 1979

Paisley collected his third Manager of the Year award in four seasons.

The Bell's award is worth £2,500 to Paisley and comes after a particularly satisfying season for Liverpool, who wrested the title back from Nottingham Forest with a record-breaking performance.

His team also collected £50,000 for scoring 84 League goals. Forest manager Brian Clough, last year's winner, received an inscribed salver and £500 for taking Forest to next Wednesday's European Cup final.

"I would like to thank the UEFA officials for delaying the European Cup final until after the voting for this award," joked Paisley.

I think any other government but the Conservative government would have given him a knighthood.

Maggie Thatcher – well you know how she used to love the miners. He was a miner's son. OBE? I would have put it in the bin. I would. Disgrace. Now a fella gets a knighthood for scoring three goals.

Our Bob had the chance to go to Real Madrid to manage in 1977 and he turned them down. He said: 'I'm happy where I am.' He wasn't

leaving Liverpool for nowt. He was a real, true fella. He was. If he made a promise, he wouldn't break that promise for anybody.

My favourite memory was everything that he did. He was fantastic, for me. He was fantastic. He did great. He was a canny lad. He's always been the same. He was never cheeky with anybody. Our Bob was just an ordinary lad. No side, nothing of that...he was just a real contented fella.

He was a great man.

BOB PAISLEY WASN'T A COLLECTOR OF THINGS. HE DIDN'T NEED TO BE. HIS FAMILY HAVE THEIR OWN PRECIOUS RECORD OF THE PUBLIC AND PRIVATE LIFE OF A FOOTBALL GENIUS

VOLUME 1

Bob's final Year as Manager. 1982-1983

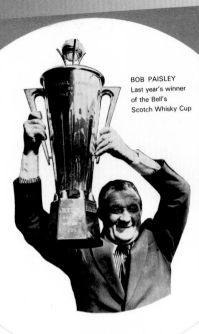

MAY 25TH 1984

BOB PRESENTED
GIFT TO
CHAIRMAN
BELLS
WHISKY

BOB PAISLEY
Last year's winner
of the Bell's
Scotch Whisky Cup

FOOTBALL MANAGERS OF THE YEAR

1968/69	Don Revie, Leeds United	F.C.
1969/70	Don Revie, Leeds United	F.C.
1970/71	Bertie Mee, Arsenal	F.C.
1971/72	Don Revie, Leeds United	F.C.
1972/73	Bill Shankly, Liverpool	F.C.
1973/74	Jack Charlton, Middlesbrough	F.C.
1974/75	Ron Saunders, Aston Villa	F.C.
1975/76	Bob Paisley, Liverpool	F.C.
1976/77	Bob Paisley, Liverpool	F.C.
1977/78	Brian Clough, Nottingham Forest	F.C.
1978/79	Bob Paisley, Liverpool	F.C.
1979/80	Bob Paisley, Liverpool	F.C.
1980/81	Ron Saunders, Aston Villa	F.C.
1981/82	Bob Paisley, Liverpool	F.C.
1982/83	Bob Paisley, Liverpool	F.C.

First Division Champions
(English record Number)
1900-01, 1905-06, 1921-22, 1922-23,
1946-47, 1963-64, 1965-66, 1972-73,
1975-76, 1976-77, 1978-79, 1979-80,
1981-82.
Second Division Champions
1893-94, 1895-96, 1904-05, 1961-62.
F.A. Cup Winners
1964-65, 1973-74.
U.E.F.A. Cup Winners
1972-73, 1975-76.
European Cup Winners
1977, 1978, 1981.
Cup Finalists
1914, 1950, 1971, 1977.
European Cup Semi-Finalists
1964-65.
European Cup Winners' Cup Finalists
1965-66.
European Fairs Cup Semi-Finalists
1970-71.
League Cup Winners
1980-81, 1981-82

With the Compliments
of
LIVERPOOL FOOTBALL
CLUB

SUPPORT YOUR CLUB

Kenny Dalglish
Bruce Grobbelaar
Bob Paisley
Phil Thompson
Joe Fagan
Graeme Souness
Ronnie Whelan
Sammy Lee
Ronnie Moran
Craig Johnston
Terry McDermott
Phil Neal
Alan Kennedy
David Hodgson

LIVERPOOL
THE ANFIELD REVIEW 35p

LIVERPOOL
THE ANFIELD REVIEW 35p

LEAGUE DIVISION 1
LIVERPOOL v.
MANCHESTER UNITED
Saturday, 16th October, 1982
Kick-off 3 p.m.

Leasowe Castle

CAROUSEL

SUNDAY AUGUST 25th.
TO AID ST. JOHN'S HOSPICE
Grand Opening by BOB PAISLEY at 12 noon

Not very 'grand'.
Poured with rain all day!

Telemessage

British TELECOM

22 APR 1983/1224

LPL0742 MRZ5418 PAH0688 P07 3398LIVE

The Red Devil Souvenir Shop
Manchester United Football Club
Old Trafford Manchester

22 April 1983

TELEMESSAGE
MR. BOB PAISLEY,
LIVERPOOL FOOTBALL CLUB,
ANFIELD,
LIVERPOOL

Heartiest congratulations on a wonderful achievement.

Your pal   Matt Busby

Telemessage

British TELECOM

13 MAY 1983/

MPA3340 GWY2871 PBE0014 ANF P14 0159WATF

Ibrox Stadium
Glasgow

13 May 1983

TELEMESSAGE LXP   GREETING-A
MR BOB PAISLEY
WATFORD FC
VICARAGE ROAD
WATFORD
HERTS

Congratulations on reaching the winning post.
You have been an outstanding example to all of us.

John Greig

Well done Bob: Two telegrams from Matt Busby and John Greig received in Bob's final season as manager

Cuttings

Two cartoons kept by the family: One (above) from the Birmingham Mail in 1982 and another, telling the story of his life as a player

Bob's Scrapbook. Number 7

AFTER

To Mark the Retirement of Mr. "Bob" Paisley, O.B.E.

The Lord Mayor of Liverpool

(Councillor Stanley Airey, O.B.E. J.P.)

requests the pleasure of the company of

MR BOB PAISLEY AND MRS PAISLEY

on Thursday, 12th May, 1983

at the Town Hall

at a Dinner

R.S.V.P.
Town Hall,
Liverpool, L2 3SW
Tel: 236 5181

PLEASE BRING THIS CARD WITH YOU

7.30 p.m. for 8.00 p.m.
Informal

THE city has basked in the reflected glory of what Liverpool football club has achieved under Mr Paisley and I felt it only right that we who represent the city should show our thanks. So said Liverpool's Lord Mayor Councillor Stanley Airey, at last night's dinner in honour of Bob Paisley, held at the Town Hall. Seventy guests were present, including representatives from all political parties as well as guests from Liverpool and Everton football clubs. Our picture shows (l. to r.): The Mayor; Mrs Jessie Paisley; Bob Paisley; and Liverpool FC chairman John Smith.

FROM THE VICE CHANCELLOR

SENATE HOUSE ABERCROMBY SQUARE P.O. BOX 147 LIVERPOOL L69 3BX

The University of Liverpool

16 December 1982

PERSONAL & CONFIDENTIAL

Dear Mr. Paisley,

BOB PAISLEY M.Sc. watches his Liverpool players in training yesterday after hearing he is to get an honorary degree from Liverpool University — But the reasons will stay secret until the ceremony.

UNIVERSITY HONOURS PAISLEY

From Daily Mail.

R. Paisley Esq., OBE
29 Bower Road
Woolton
Liverpool L25 4RG

LIVERPOOL F.C. SCHOOL OF SCIENCE

Bob Paisley Master of Science—official

By Echo Reporter

Celebrating with a cuppa ... Bob Paisley at Melwood to-day.

From Liverpool Ec

1983

By JIM REHILL
Jan. 1983

Bob's Scrapbook
No. 9

"ROBERT PAISLEY, O.B.E.,
HE WAS MADE AN M.Sc.,
THOUGH A MODEST MAN
IS HE,
TAUGHT THEM ALL A THING
— OR THREE!"

10

C 44

Bob signs for law

I'VE got your number . . . Bob Paisley gives his signature to eager autograph hunters at Hetton Park when even the law joined the queue.

Policewoman Julie Baines told Bob she wanted his signature for a colleague's son and that she supported Sunderland.

Bob was in Hetton at the weekend to unveil a plaque at Dees Supermarket in Front Street to mark his achievement as manager of Liverpool and then went on to re-open Hetton Park.

More pictures and full report . . . Page 3.

Paisley heads return of yesterday's soccer stars

Watching Liverpool 'greatest gift of lif

BOB UNVEILS PLAQUE IN HIS HONOUR. HETTON. 23RD JULY 1983

Unveiling a plaque in his honour during a visit to his home town Hetton (left). Volume 2 cover (above) and various cuttings from 1983 (below)

BOB UNVEILS PLAQUE TO REOPEN PARK. JULY 23 1983

LIVERPOOL FOOTBALL CLUB
AND ATHLETIC GROUNDS P.L.C.
ANFIELD ROAD, LIVERPOOL L4 0TH

Thursday, 22nd September, 1983

Retirement Dinner for Mr. & Mrs. Paisley - 6.45 p.m. for 7.15 p.m. Note revised time - Directors and Wives.

Dinner

given by

THE LORD MAYOR OF LIVERPOOL

(Councillor Stanley Airey, O.B.E., J.P.)

at the

One more unusual item in the scrapbooks is a signed Ulster bank note (see below)

PRESENTS (ROYAL DOULTON) GIVEN BY DIRECTORS OF L.F.C.

Bob's their 'Uncle'

LIVERPOOL'S retired big-winner boss BOB PAISLEY is wanted at Nottingham Forest, Southampton and Mid-dlesbrough.

The three top-name bosses—BRIAN CLOUGH, LAWRIE McMENEMY and MALCOLM ALLI-SON—have invited him to watch their players at all levels and observe their systems.

"If I spot something different, then I'll be at liberty to offer them my opinion," he says, "I'll probably take them up on their kind offers.

"A word of warning, though. Wily Bob is scouting weekly for Liverpool and would, no doubt, report any good findings to manager JOE FAGAN.

FROM SUNDAY MIRROR Oct. 23rd 1983.

Yorkshire Executive Sporting Club
BOXING DINNER EVENING

at the Norfolk Gardens Hotel, Bradford on Monday 3rd October 1983

IN HONOUR OF
BOB PAISLEY O.B.E.
THE MOST SUCCESSFUL FOOTBALL MANAGER OF ALL TIME

IN RECOGNITION OF HIS OUTSTANDING CONTRIBUTION TO THE WORLD OF SOCCER.

BANK LIMITED 10

C4419017

BANK LIMITED PROMISE TO PAY THE BEARER ON DEMAND

N POUNDS 10

OR ULSTER BANK LIMITED

CHIEF EXECUTIVE

£10 NOTE AUTOGRAPHED BY CHIEF EXECUTIVE

LIVERPOOL F.C. 83/84

Volume 6

CENTENARY FOOTBALL MATCH

ON WEDNESDAY THE 19th OF NOVEMBER

Kick off 7.30pm

BISHOP AUCKLAND from:-

TONY HARRISON
MALLY NEWTON
ALAN BARKER
DAVID VARTY
WILSON BLAIR
PAUL BROWN
LEE REDHEAD
GARY LORMOR
COLIN BLACKBURN
ANDY TOMAN
PHIL LINACRE
JOHN GRADY
PETER HINDS
MARK LAWRENCE
WARREN PEARSON
DAVID CALLAGHAN

Colours:-
TWO BLUES

LIVERPOOL from:-

MIKE HOOPER
IAN TOALE
GARY ABLETT
MARK SEAGRAVES
ALEX WATSON
JOHN McGREGOR
KEN DE MANGE
IAN FAIRBROTHER
STEVE STAUNTON
JIM MAGILTON
JOHN JEFFERS
WAYNE HARRISON
JOHN DURNIN
BRIAN MOONEY
SEAN CURRY

Colours:-
ALL RED

Autographs of some ex-players and others whom Bob knew.

Referee:- Mr. R.A. HART (Darlington)

Linesman:- Mr. T. PARK (Darlington)
Mr. R. CARR (Ferryhill)

April 19th

With Kay Kelly at Gold Medal Luncheon

MERSEYSIDE ACHIEVEMENT MEDAL
LPA

TYNESIDE SUMMER FESTIVAL.

From Liverpool Echo. Thurs. March 31st 1983

Received April 6th 1983

Bob set to net Freeman accolade

By Peter Phelps

LIVERPOOL'S Bob Paisley stands poised to win the ultimate Scouse accolade.

Moves are under way to make Bob the first Freeman since 1970 — Liberal Councillor Richard Kemp — said today: "I am sure this will be supported by all sides of the council — even by Evertonians."

The last person to receive the top honour was Littlewoods founder Sir John Moores, a former chairman of Everton F.C.

But the procedure of creating Freemen disappeared from Liverpool Council's rule book following local government re-organisation in 1974.

So at the next meeting of the council Councillor Kemp will try to change the rules so that Bob Paisley and others who have "conspicuously worked for the good of the City of Liverpool and its citizens," can be honoured.

"Being a Freeman is a singular honour," said Councillor Kemp. "And it is appropriate that I should move this because I am the only member of Liverpool Council who is not interested in football.

"But Bob Paisley has given the people of this city a reason to hold their heads up high

---

THE DECADE

A poem in honour of my Liverpool friends by Wolfgang Jähnig (IN DRESDEN)

Wherever I wander wherever I use to be
I'll never forget March 21 in 1973.
The way led me directly to the Neva Hotel,
to be honest first a little apprehensive I felt.
I looked and finally I found
Bill Shankly, Bob Paisley and their backroom staff
at a table around.
They asked me to take a seat,
I was so glad to have them ever met.
The European Cup took the Reds to Dresden twice over again,
the friendship has grown more and more since then.
From now on we've never seen ones more
so in the following years from here I listened
to the phantastic roar.
If at Anfield, Old Trafford, Wembley or on the Continent,
You should have heard beat my heart for my favourite team,
it was reality and no dream the great success all over the years,
with joy my eyes were sometimes filled with tears.
How many times I jumped up,
when a goal was scored in the Champs or Cup.
How much I could mention what I often dream
of Bob, his family, his friends and his team.
You can't imagine what I've done so much
for Liverpool at school, among friends with whom I was in touch.
Now after Bob has decided to retire,
I must say what I especially admire.
His greatness, patience and ever friendly manner,
last but not least his lifelong being together
with one Club for more than 40 years.
Let's lift the glasses and say "Three Cheers".
Keep in good condition in your future life,
do spend a lot of yours furthermore with your sympathetic wife.
She must be included in your great success,
teaching, housekeeping, understanding soccer, oh yes.
May be continued what you've built up
and follow more Champs successes and Cup by Cup.

COUNCIL SUMMONS

(NOTE: Your attendance at the commencement of the Meeting is particularly requested, since the Resolution to be submitted to the Council, sitting as a Special Council, will not be effective unless it is passed by not less than two-thirds of the Members of the Council voting thereon.

CITY OF LIVERPOOL

City Solicitor's Office, Municipal Buildings, Liverpool L69 2DH.
22nd July, 1983.

Dear Sir/Madam,

You are requested to attend a Meeting of the City Council to be held on Wednesday next, the 27th July, 1983, at 1.30 p.m. at the Town Hall, as a Special Council under Section 249 of the Local Government Act 1972.

Yours faithfully,

City Solicitor,
Secretary to the Council.

To all Members of the City Council.

AGENDA

I.—MINUTES of the meeting of the City Council held on 29th June 1983

II.—HONORARY FREEDOM OF THE CITY

To consider a resolution of the Policy and Finance Committee of 19th July 1983, recommending, pursuant to section 249 of the Local Government Act 1972, that—

(i) in pursuance of the Local Government Act 1972, the Honorary Freedom of the City of Liverpool be conferred upon Mr. Robert Paisley, O.B.E., in recognition of the eminent service rendered by him to the City in his achievements with Liverpool Football Club; and

(ii) the Chief Executive, after consultation with the Chairman of that Committee, be authorised to make the necessary arrangements arising from resolution (i) above and that authority be granted for the payment of the expenditure involved.

(NOTE.—A resolution of the Council to comply with the Act must be passed by not less than two-thirds of the Members voting thereon at a meeting of the Council specially convened for this purpose.)

Paisley freedom vote a winner

FORMER Liverpool football club manager, Bob Paisley is to be awarded the city's highest honour.

At a special meeting yesterday councillors overwhelmingly voted to give the Freedom of the City to the ex-Reds boss.

Council leader John Hamilton said Mr Paisley had brought great credit to the city and it was right to honour someone who had brought expertise, enthusiasm and integrity to the Anfield club.

Mr Paisley, OBE, who joined the club as a player in 1939 joined the backroom staff in 1953 and worked his way up from assistant trainer to club manager.

Councillor Hamilton said: "Mr Paisley has achieved outstanding individual success in his chosen career. Thereby bringing great credit to our city.

"His influence goes much wider than the confines of Anfield or indeed the football world — he had a significant effect upon his adopted city and its citizens.

The special ceremony at which the honour will be bestowed on Mr Paisley will be held later this year.

Mr Paisley was not at the meeting — he was attending a retirement party in his birthplace at Hetton-le-Hole, Tyne and Wear.

However, his sons Robert (34) and Graham (32), were there and Graham said: "My father was deeply honoured.

"This is a tribute that is only bestowed on a few people and all the family are very appreciative."

Earlier this month, Mr Paisley received an Honorary Master of Science degree from Liverpool University.

Bob's Scrapbook Number 8

BOB PAISLEYS LAST MATCH AT WATFORD

Graham →   Mum →

Signing off ... old campaigner Bob Paisley surrounded by young fans, at Watford.

From Liverpool Daily Post. May 16th 1983

Bob's final team sheet

by Nick Hilton

BOB PAISLEY wrote out the last team sheet of his career as a First Division manager yesterday.

And typically it was an unchanged line-up that he pencilled in to take Liverpool's championship bow at Watford today.

Paisley saw signs in the morning training session that his players are in the mood to sign off the season on a winning note and end a sequence of four defeats and two draws since the title was effectively clinched almost a month ago.

"My memory is getting bad, I can't even remember the last time we won a match," Paisley joked last night.

But he added: "I really won't know it is all over until the first game of next season. A lot will depend on how I am going to be

involved in the future."

That role could even be in the Liverpool boardroom. The club will announce its plans for the future when Paisley and the team return from Israel later this month.

In the meantime, striker David Fairclough will be allowed to leave the club, possibly on a free transfer.

Watford manager Graham Taylor will interrupt his England Youth squad duties to be in charge of his side today.

With midfielder Les Taylor the only injury absentee, he has a full senior squad from which to make a late decision on his line-up.

LIVERPOOL: Grobbelaar, Neal, Kennedy, Thompson, Lawrenson, Hansen, Dalglish, Lee, Hodgson, Johnstone, Souness. Sub: Nicol.

⚽ Watford

FOOTBALL LEAGUE DIVISION ONE

Saturday, 14th May, 1983

LIVERPOOL

Kick-off 3.00 pm
at Vicarage Road Stadium

ADMIT TO DIRECTORS' BOX and GUEST SUITE.

E. Plumley, Chief Executive

SEAT No. B   4

News of Liverpool from Thailand !!

BANGKOK POST THURSDAY APRIL 21, 1983

SPORTS POST

Liverpool clinch League title

LONDON — Liverpool clinched the English League soccer title for the 14th time Tuesday — without kicking a ball.

Arch-rival Everton's 2-0 win over Manchester United means that United cannot now exceed Liverpool's current point total of 81 — it can only tie with it — but Liverpool has a vastly superior goal difference than the FA Cup finalist.

Liverpool would have to lose its remaining five matches and concede 31 goals more than it scores for United to win the title — and United would have to win its last seven

matches.

That possibility is so unlikely that further discussion of its eventuality is meaningless.

ON COURSE

Everton kept on course for Europe with goals from Graeme Sharp (64th) and Adrian Heath (71st). Aston Villa also

...ons all over
...d: News of
... title victory
...nced in
... (top).
...vitations to
...n where
...eys rubbed
...s with
...elow right:
... scrapbook
...er he quit
...eld

In Honour of Their Royal Highnesses The Duke and Duchess of York

The Chairman of Liverpool City Council
(Councillor Thomas McManus, J.P.)
requests the pleasure of the company of

Mrs. Paisley

on Friday, 12th

at the To

at a L

Town Hall,
Liverpool L2 3SW
Tel: 236 5181

Friday Feb. 12th 1988
Town Hall.
Met. Duke and Duchess of York.

In Honour of Their Royal Highnesses The Duke and Duchess of York

The Chairman of Liverpool City Council
(Councillor Thomas McManus, J.P.)
requests the pleasure of the company of

Mr. R. Paisley O.B.E.

on Friday, 12th February, 1988,

at the Town Hall

at a Luncheon

12.00 p.m.
for
1.00 p.m.
Dress: Lounge Suit

LUNCHEON

given by

THE CHAIRMAN OF LIVERPOOL CITY COUNCIL
(Councillor Thomas McManus, J.P.)

at the

TOWN HALL, LIVERPOOL

on

Bob's final Scrapbook after retiring from the Board

WHSMITH
Recycled P

BOB FOLLOWS A FILM STAR

THE LAST time someone was singled out for the honour of making their very own Royal Doulton plate, during a visit to the famous Potteries factory, that person was a film star . . . Judy Garland . . . which is why this picture makes Liverpool manager Bob Paisley someone rather special, too, because he followed in the American star's footsteps, as it were.

As the inscription on the dish says, it was made by Bob during his visit to the Royal Doulton factory at Burslem and presented to him (inset picture) as a memento of his visit. The presentation was made before our European Cup-tie against Dundalk.

From "Anfield Review" - Oct 26th 1982

ספורט חדשות

פייזל: 20 תארים ב־פ שנים
(עמ' 28*29)

WELLCOME BOB

From Jewish Paper

Bob with Avi Cohen

LIVERPOOL TELEPHONE AREA MAGAZINE

Summer 1983

No. 150

Crown Paints Presentation.

P.T.O

Paisley salute a real treasure

FORTY-FOUR years is a long time — so it's not surprising that Liverpool manager Bob Paisley relishes the chance to recall some of his early Anfield feats in the Echo's superb souvenir publication in his honour.

Paisley recalling some of his golden days in our special edition

And that nostalgic moment, when he scored the winner against Everton in the F.A. Cup to put his side through to the final, is but one of many dramatic moments it captures.

Also recalled in the Echo's Salute to Bob Paisley are some of the great players of the past — Stubbins, Liddell, Balmer and company — who are pictured in their heyday and also a colourful club reunion a few years ago.

Era of

Liverpool slip up

BENNIE TABAK was the toast of Israel's soccer fans yesterday after scoring all the national squad's goals in a 4-3 victory over Liverpool in a friendly international in Tel Aviv.

He scored in the 15th, 20th, 60th and 85th minutes.

Liverpool's star striker Kenny Dalglish replied in the 21st minute and substitute Jim McGregor scored in the 76th and 89th minutes.

The crowd of 25,000 gave a standing ovation to Liverpool manager Bob Paisley after he was presented with a commemorative trophy at half time.

Liverpool: Grobbelaar, Neal, Hansen, Thompson, Kennedy, Nicol, Johnston, Lee, Dalglish, Hodgson (McGregor), Souness.

From Daily Post May 17th.

Top left: Following in Judy Garland's footsteps! Above: A spelling mistake but it's the thought that counts in this front page from a 'Jewish paper'. Left: More cuttings from Israel visit and (below) a game of snooker with advice from professionals Ray Reardon and Doug Mountjoy

BEHIND
every great manager

BOB QUITE SIMPLY COULDN'T HAVE ACHIEVED WHAT HE DID WITHOUT HIS LOYAL AND LOVING WIFE JESSIE. THEIR PARTNERSHIP WAS THE ROCK ON WHICH BOB BUILT HIS EMPIRE

> As Liverpool prepared for the 1979-80 season, it was a case of fine tuning rather than a new engine as far as summer reorganisation was concerned. Liverpool were still the masters with Anfield a place where opposition goals were few and far between. Paisley was in his pomp, supported by a strong backroom team with the fans confident in his abilities to continue the glory years

1979-80

Champs see Double dreams dashed again

It was the 100th official season of competitive football in England, which began with the Reds seeing off Arsenal 3-1 in the traditional curtain-raiser to the season, the FA Charity Shield at Wembley. Avi Cohen was the only summer signing while Emlyn Hughes joined Wolves, although young prospect Ronnie Whelan was brought in before September was out.

Another League Championship also suggested Liverpool could maintain their domestic dominance well into the new decade (again secured with victory over Aston Villa). The Reds' nearest challengers were Manchester United (who finished two points behind with an inferior goal difference), although their European Cup bid was ended by Dynamo Tbilisi in round one – Nottingham Forest ending up retaining the trophy. Terry McDermott scooped both the PFA and the Footballer Writers' Player of the Year awards (he scored 16 goals that season).

The Reds' Double bid was again ended at the semi-final stage, holders Arsenal winning after a third FA Cup replay while hopes of a first-ever League Cup success were dashed by Nottingham Forest, who won through to face Wolves courtesy of a 2-1 aggregate success.

Kenny Dalglish was again an ever-present alongside Phil Neal

JESSIE'S STORY

Jessie: With a precious memento of Bob – his famous flat cap

JESSIE Paisley enjoyed a remarkable journey with her Bob. The two met aboard a midnight train to London after soldier Bob entered her carriage and promptly dropped his army overcoat on her sandwiches. She told him off and the two got talking. A bond was formed and the pair were together for the rest of their lives.

Their journey together ended in 1996 but not before Bob had guided Liverpool to an historic and unsurpassed haul of silverware and Jessie had raised a family of two boys and a girl while forging her own successful career as a Primary School teacher.

The secret to their success was, like Bob's philisophy on the game he loved, keeping things simple. Jessie accepted that her private time with Bob would be limited because of the devotion to his job. Family holidays were planned but often had to be shelved because of football commitments. She has, like all devoted mothers, kept mementoes and photos of family celebrations and happy times together. Unlike other mothers, though, there is often a figure missing on the faded pictures of summer holidays – Bob, again, called away from the family in the line of Anfield duty. "I came second to football but truly, I never resented it," she revealed in an interview in 1992.

Still living in the house they shared in the Liverpool suburb of Woolton, Jessie's memories of Bob are bright and her recollections vivid. She still attends her local church of St Peter's, where Bob is buried – with one of his caps – and her son Graham works.

Midnight meeting with Bob's dad – fresh from the pit!

Early days: In 1949 after Robert was born

B ob was getting ready to make his official first team debut for Liverpool when he took me to see his family in Hetton.

We didn't arrive until midnight and when we got there, Bob's dad came downstairs. He'd just come in from the pit. It was funny, landing there and meeting your future in-laws in the middle of the night.

I was a bit nervous but Bob's mum was awfully kind. His dad was more brusque but he was lovely and he absolutely adored the children when they were little. He wasn't given to saying anything, not given to lots of emotions. He was a nice man, his dad, not very talkative, a bit like Bob.

His mum was a lovely person. She was ever so kind.

➤

➤ (the duo playing 60 games), as was Phil Thompson while Graeme Souness and Ray Clemence missed only one league game. David Johnson would be top scorer, with 27 goals in all competitions with Dalglish notching 23.

Despite this prolific form, Paisley would bring in a young Chester City striker who had been making an impression in the lower divisions late on in the campaign. His name was Ian Rush.

My all-time greats

**Liverpool Echo
September 22, 1979**

As part of his 'Liverpool Scrapbook' (Souvenir Press) he names a side he would like to have played in – possibly against a Rest of the World side. He named the following XI (to play in a 4-3-3 formation):

Ray Clemence
Bill Jones ("I couldn't leave him out, and that would have been his best position")
Ron Yeats ("A must")
Tommy Smith ("Commanded a place somewhere")
Emlyn Hughes
Phil Taylor
Kevin Keegan
Bill Shankly
Kenny Dalglish
Roger Hunt
Bill Liddell
Sub:
Ian St John

Smith was made captain ahead of Taylor: "While he said his piece and sometimes slagged team-mates even when he himself was not having a particularly good game, he still had the drive, that capability to gee up others. Yes, they knew when Tommy was having an off-day, but they still responded to his nagging, driving, arguing – call it what you will – because, I believe, they recognised that above all, whether playing well or not, he was giving no less than 100 per cent every time. And for that he commended their respect and got the response he was seeking."

On Bill Shankly, he added: "He had an uncanny influence on his players. He may not have had any degrees in psychology, but he was the best brain-washer I've ever encountered. He used to make the players feel like giants and opponents almost like pygmies."

Paisley criticises the old masters

From cutting October 5, 1979

Paisley laid down the law In the wake of the European Cup defeat to Dynamo Tbilisi:

"It's going to take a lot of hard work, and I don't just mean for the players. I'm sure we have a team which can perform at Lord Mayors' Shows, but we have to do bread and butter work as well, and that is important.

"We have got to get it organised now because every game is a cup final. Great teams score goals. It's no use looking good and not producing the goods at the end. We knock it around but when we get up there we are like a powder puff.

"If you are like that you are only a moderate team. I am not just talking about the two men at the front, although I am not exonerating them. Everyone in this side has responsibility.

"We have build-ups taking six to seven moves to get there but then we get carried away with the music. The music soothes us when we should have the explosion."

Cheers! It's Bob's vintage win

Liverpool Echo, January 5, 1980

A 100 per cent record in December – seven games, seven wins – has boosted Liverpool manager Bob Paisley to the

Home values: Bob's Mum and Dad

The women, of course, did everything in those days. They decorated the house every year. It was a pit house so it got sooty but they never took the paper off, they put another roll on, so it must have been an inch thick by the time I went there. It was a nice little place Hetton. You wouldn't know it now because all the houses in Downs Lane where he lived were pit houses.

They've all been re-done with porches put outside. They've all had toilets put in; they were outside before.

There was a big tin bath on the wall. There were no pit baths at the beginning when I went there and they used to have to clear everybody out while the dad came home and had his bath in front of the fire at night, all sooty.

Visiting: At Downs Lane with Jessie and Robert in June, 1949

'THE WOMEN DID EVERYTHING IN THOSE DAYS. THEY DECORATED THE HOUSE. IT WAS A PIT HOUSE SO IT GOT SOOTY BUT THEY NEVER TOOK THE PAPER OFF, THEY PUT ANOTHER ROLL ON, SO IT MUST HAVE BEEN AN INCH THICK'

Manager of the Month award against stiff opposition.

His team's great run of success, as they replaced Manchester United in top place, ensured him getting the award in the voting of a panel of football writers, above Southampton's Lawrie McMenemy and Brighton's Alan Mullery.

Bob's team talk wakes coma boy

**From cutting
April 7, 1980**

A 14-year-old soccer fan who had been in a coma for seven days is on the mend – thanks to Bob Paisley.

Richard Bean was admitted to the intensive care unit of a Sheffield hospital after suffering head injuries in a car accident.

He lay there unconscious for over a week until striking workmates at a British Steel plant where his father Fred is a crane driver, decided to get in touch with the Liverpool chief and ask for his help.

They held a series of collections and two of them travelled to Anfield – home of Richard's soccer heroes.

They came back with a taped message from the Liverpool chief and when it was played to Richard he opened his eyes for the first time.

Now his parents say there has been a dramatic change in Richard's condition and they think it is only a matter of time before he makes a full recovery.

"All I did was introduce myself on the tape and say that I hoped he would soon be well.

"It is absolutely terrific news that the lad is on the road to recovery," said Paisley.

When Richard is fully better Mr Paisley has invited him to spend a day at the club.

"He will be made most welcome at Anfield.

"We will give him a tour of the ground," he added.

1980-81

League woe masked by Treble glory

Three points for a win was introduced prior to the new campaign, and it would be Bob Paisley's least successful – in the league at least.

Liverpool, dogged by injury, slipped to fifth, their lowest First Division finish for 10 years with a poor away record and a total of 17 draws accounting for the disappointment. January 31st, 1981 also saw the club's impressive three-year unbeaten run ended by Leicester City, a run of 85 games in all competitions. There was also the disappointment of a fourth-round exit to Everton in the FA Cup.

Despite this, there would be three more additions to an already cluttered trophy room at Anfield. Having beaten West Ham United in the FA Charity Shield, the Hammers would also be beaten in the League Cup, the Reds claiming a first-ever triumph in the competition, 2-1 in a replay at Villa Park.

The icing on the cake proved to be in the European Cup where a third success was secured, courtesy of a 1-0 win over Real Madrid in Paris. Amongst the notable games in that run would be the first round, second leg clash with part-timers Oulu Palloseura. Having only drawn 1-1 away in the first game in Finland, Paisley's men eased to a 10-1 triumph. Aberdeen and CSKA Sofia were swept aside before the semi-final against Bayern Munich. Following a 0-0 draw at Anfield, the Germans had printed details of how to get to Paris for the final ahead of the second leg. But against all odds, a weakened Liverpool team would reach the French capital. Early on Kenny Dalglish was forced off injured but his substitute Howard Gayle proved a more than able replacement, causing all sorts of problems before being brought off for Jimmy Case.

We should have been at this ✓

The Prime Minister
and Mr. Denis Thatcher

request the honour of the company of

Mr and Mrs Robert Paisley

at a Reception at 10, Downing Street, Whitehall
on Monday, 9th May, 1983, from 6.30 p.m. to 8.00 p.m.

An answer is requested to:
The Secretary (Invitations),
10, Downing Street, Whitehall

But Bob had previously arranged to do th

Off to Downing Street at second time of asking . . . but Bob hated it

ANGLO-AMERICAN SPORTING CLUB
(MANCHESTER)

BOXING-DINNER EVENING
IN HONOUR OF

BOB PAISLEY, O.B.E.
HOTEL PICCADILLY, MANCHESTER
MONDAY, 9th MAY, 1983
DINNER 7.30 p.m. PROMPT
Peacock Bar open for Members and Guests 6.30 p.m. to 1 a.m.

Double booked! A page from Jessie's scrapbook

I remember when we first got an invitation to go and see the Prime Minister after Bob retired in 1983. We couldn't go. Bob had already arranged to go to a boxing dinner on the same evening and he'd given his word that he'd go.

We did eventually go to 10 Downing Street during Margaret Thatcher's time, but it was a dead loss for Bob.

He said that he didn't know how we had got on the list and that her secretary must have had a space on the end and put our name in it. It was one of those days when you are standing up all the time and Bob didn't like it. We went up that famous big staircase with all the pictures of former Prime Ministers on the walls.

Bob said to Mrs. Thatcher 'Don't forget, whenever you come to Liverpool you will be welcome at Anfield.' I don't think she was listening or interested in football. I found the day quite an experience, but Bob called it a 'duty' to attend and nothing more. I enjoyed the experience and still have the ticket.

Reserves Colin Irwin and Richard Money were inspired in defence and despite striker David Johnson hobbling on the wing, he would set up Ray Kennedy for the all-important away goal seven minutes from time – which proved decisive after the Germans equalised late on. Indeed it would be the other Kennedy, Alan, who would prove the toast of the Parc des Princes.

Phil Neal was the only ever-present, while Ray Clemence, Ray Kennedy and Terry McDermott all made 60 appearances or more – the latter top-scoring with 22 goals in all competitions.

There had been little transfer activity in the first half of the season, with the only major change being the signing of goalkeeper Bruce Grobbelaar from Vancouver Whitecaps in March. His arrival would signal the departure of Ray Clemence at the end of the season, with the only other major moves being the incoming Craig Johnston in April, with Steve Heighway leaving for Minnesota Kicks.

Nostalgic reunion for Bob

From cutting December 1, 1980

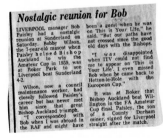

Nostalgic reunion for Bob

LIVERPOOL manager Bob Paisley had a nostalgic reunion at Sunderland on Saturday. Bobby Wilson, the 7-year-old mascot when Paisley helped Bishop Auckland to win the Amateur Cup in 1939, was at Roker Park to see Liverpool beat Sunderland 4-2.

Wilson, now a council maintenance worker, had closely followed Paisley's career but has never met him since that great Bishop Auckland triumph.

"I corresponded with Bob when I was abroad in the RAF and might have been a guest when he was on This is Your Life," he said. "But our paths have not crossed since the good old days with the Bishops.

"I was disappointed when ITV could not find me to appear on 'This is Your Life'. I even missed Bob when he came back to Hetton-le-Hole with the European Cup."

It was at Roker that Bishop Auckland beat Willington in the FA Amateur Cup final. Paisley, the son of a County Durham miner, signed for Liverpool straight after the match.

Liverpool manager Bob Paisley had a nostalgic reunion at Sunderland on Saturday. Bobby Wilson, the seven-year-old mascot when Paisley helped Bishop Auckland to win the Amateur Cup in 1939, was at Roker Park to see Liverpool beat Sunderland 4-2.

Wilson has never met him since that great Bishop Auckland triumph.

Here's your degree

➤
"I corresponded with Bob when I was abroad in the RAF and might have been a guest when he was on This Is Your Life. But our paths have not crossed since the good old days with the Bishops.

"I was disappointed when ITV could not find me to appear on This Is Your Life. I even missed Bob when he came back to Hetton-le-Hole with the European Cup."

Mr Incredible as calm as ever

Liverpool Daily Post, May 28, 1981

Football's Mr Incredible was as calm and matter of fact as ever amid the popping champagne corks at the Parc des Princes Stadium last night.

Paisley had just engineered the defeat of the famous Real Madrid in the European Cup final and it can only silence the battery of critics who believe they are over the hill.

Yet the quiet North Easterner was almost apologetic that the game had not provided the showpiece football to match the occasion.

"Maybe we have won things with better performances but we showed a lot of character. Without the injuries, I feel we would have been closer to the title."

1981-82

World first as Rush inspires more glory

The Reds made up for the previous season's First Division blip by reclaiming the crown, their 13th top-flight title.

Paisley's men held off the challenge of Ipswich Town by four points, scoring 80 goals in the process. It was a tricky first half of the season, with Paisley relieving Phil Thompson of the captaincy following a 3-1 home defeat to Manchester City on Boxing Day (which left the Reds in 12th), to be replaced by Graeme ➤

First class: Family snap of the graduation day

Bob's achievements were one day recognised by Liverpool University who decided to give him an honorary degree.

On the script they sent us, it indicated that when he went up to collect his scroll he should not wear his cap. Bob thought they meant his flat cap! He didn't think he would be going up wearing a mortar board and gown. The chap who was making the presentation used this in his quote.

Of course, Bob's flat caps were his trademark, although I don't know where those stories came from suggesting he sometimes went to work in his cardigan and slippers. That was not true. That was just one of the things invented by the press.

Yes, he wore a cardigan, but I never saw him go out in slippers. It's one of those little stories that grows with time.

I actually got him to wear his cap because he was thinning on top. One day I wanted to take him into town because I felt he needed a new cap.

Bob objected strongly. 'Why do we have to go?' he complained. He hated shopping. I got him that new one but I doubt if he ever wore it. He was comfortable in his old one.

I still have some of Bob's old caps now. One is probably still in the boot of my car, always reminding me of him.

but forget the cap!

Back in cap and gown for a club honour with Alan Hansen in 1988 and (below) with Robert Runcie, the Archbishop of Canterbury in 1983

'ONE DAY I WANTED TO TAKE HIM INTO TOWN BECAUSE I FELT HE NEEDED A NEW CAP. BOB OBJECTED STRONGLY. 'WHY DO WE HAVE TO GO?' HE COMPLAINED. HE HATED SHOPPING. I GOT HIM THAT NEW ONE. BUT I DOUBT IF HE EVER WORE IT'

Souness. The idea was aimed to release the pressure on his defender, with the captaincy affecting his form according to Bob:

"My reason for the decision was that I felt Phil had been going through a rough patch playing-wise and I thought the extra responsibility of leading the team was having an effect."

The following game Swansea City were beaten 4-0 in the FA Cup. The Reds did not look back, losing only three other games in all competitions, a run which included 11 consecutive league wins.

There was to be a second consecutive League Cup too, Tottenham Hotspur (who the Reds also beat to confirm the title) being defeated 3-1 at Wembley after extra time after Ronnie Whelan had equalised late on. Phil Neal recalled:

"Paisley would not let us sit down before extra time started. He was bellowing: 'Get up on your feet, don't let them see you are tired.'

"It stemmed from Shankly, who would never let an opponent see that you were weak. After that, we felt we had it in the bag."

But the FA Cup would again elude Paisley, Liverpool going down 2-0 at Chelsea in round five while there would be defeat in the European Cup quarter-finals to CSKA Sofia.

However, the season would be overshadowed somewhat by the death of Bill Shankly on September 29, 1981, at the age of 68.

Mark Lawrenson became the most expensive defender in Britain when he signed for Liverpool from Brighton in August for £900,000, with the fee recouped over the course of the season with sales including Jimmy Case, Ray Kennedy, Colin Irwin and Avi Cohen. The other notable signing was a 20-year-old from Ayr United – Steve Nicol.

Of the 62 games played Bruce Grobbelaar, Kenny Dalglish and Phil Neal played in every one. Ian Rush announced his arrival as a

> player of some promise by plundering 30 goals in 49 games, with Dalglish (22), Terry McDermott (20) and another youngster Ronnie Whelan (14) all making their mark. Bob would secure a fifth Bell's Manager of the Year crown.

The season was also marked by a first-ever appearance in the World Club Championship. As reigning European champions, Liverpool faced the South American winners Flamengo in Japan. However, inspired by Zico, the Brazilians eased to a 3-0 victory in December.

Who's a playboy?

**Liverpool Echo
September 14, 1981**

Speaking after the 2-0 defeat at Ipswich Town (meaning Liverpool had picked up only four points from 12), Paisley said: "They have got to be professional not playboys or fly-by-nights."

But Neal, who scored an own goal in that game, responded: "I can understand him talking about the attitude. There are obviously things wrong but I think we are as professional as we have ever been. Perhaps we could do with some of the Tommy Smith attitude.

"Obviously we have had a bad start so perhaps the boss thought he had to say something. But you can't be good professionals one year and playboys and fly-by-nights the next.

"It's been a bad enough week for the England lads in the team (they lost in Norway) without being called playboys at the end

Tough keeping a TV secret for three months

The famous final scene of Bob's This Is Your Life programme in 1977

When Bob was picked to appear on the TV series 'This Is Your Life' we had to keep the secret for three months. Bob was away when they contacted us and asked if we would take part. All the family and many of his friends had to keep the secret all that time which was hard. Of course, Liverpool Football Club and the players all knew about it, but nothing came out. The club had won the European Cup and Bob was taking it up to Hetton in the North East to show it to his old friends. When he came back he said that many had been missing, but that was because they'd been told to keep away because they were due to surprise him on 'This Is Your Life'.

of it. In fact, it's been a nightmare week. But when the public read the word 'playboy' they get all kinds of ideas.

"Most of the team are married men with responsibilities. If the boss did not mean that, he should not have said it."

Paisley subsequently expanded on his original comment:

"When I talk about playboys and fly-by-nights, I am talking about the attitude. The players just seem to be saying sorry and think it's over and done with. They will have to change their attitude."

Five divisions a must – Paisley

From cutting January 16, 1982

Opinion taken on the eve of the draw for the 1982 World Cup finals, and the prospect of the season running beyond May 22 – the date of the FA Cup final:

"I think we will be forced into extending the season, and the international teams just won't get the time they want for preparation," said Paisley

"I don't see any answer other than cutting the number of fixtures down and the only way of doing that is cutting down the number of teams in each division and making five leagues instead of the present four. That way no club has to go out of the League and there might be room for the likes of Altrincham, who deserve a place in the Football League."

Paisley suggested First and Second Divisions of 18 teams with the other three regionalised.

And one way of making the transition as painless as possible would be to reduce the First Division by one club for each of the next four years.

Paisley added: "There is too much football as it is and, while the smaller clubs say they need as many games as possible, their gates are suffering more than anyone's.

"People will say it's fine for Bob Paisley to advocate smaller

divisions and fewer competitions because Liverpool are successful and have the extra games.

"But you have to make people hungry for football again. If you have a good game and then wait a week, people are gasping for the next one. There are simply too many games at the moment and people can't afford to come to them."

Paisley on Ray Kennedy

**Liverpool Echo,
By Ken Rogers
January 27, 1982**

"He did a tremendous job for us. It was one of the best moves I have ever made dropping him back into midfield. He was under-rated by the fans. In fact, the European people probably recognised his talents more than the people at home. There is no doubt that Ray was one of our key men.

"He had excellent control. When he first came here he got his weight down and he has always looked after himself. He's got control, vision and excellent distribution.

"In the penalty area, I rated him as good as anyone I know. He was always a threat to opponents and when he moved into the box he could be lethal. Ray always showed exceptional positional sense. He didn't have to charge around like smaller people.

"I was sorry to lose him, but the time was right. Some people said he was slow, but he was rarely exposed."

Yobbos: It's only a few, says Bob

**Liverpool Echo
By Nick Hilton
March 22, 1982**

Bob Paisley last night explained his bitter rebuke to the Anfield crowd on Saturday following the storm over Craig Johnston's substitution.

Surprise! Bob is caught on the team coach . . .

With Jessie and brother Hughie with wife Mary

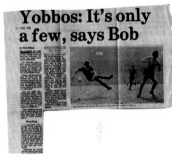

Anfield guests – Shanks and Billy Liddell

> The decision was greeted by widespread booing and heckling from a small section of the 30,000 crowd.

Paisley said immediately after the game that his reasons for taking off Johnston, making only his second full League appearance for Liverpool, were: "Too intelligent for some of the yobbos in the crowd to understand."

Yobbos: It's only a few, says Bob

And last night the Anfield boss added: "When I referred to yobbos I was only talking about three or four people. Everyone is entitled to his opinion but when it gets personal as it did on this occasion in the case of three or four people, it is different.

"They turned on me and I know where they sit and who they are if they are there next time. I don't want to label everyone with it.

"I explained why I brought Craig Johnston off. He was probably the freshest man we had out there but he is also difficult to read. It was nothing against the lad but I was trying to save the other 10 players by bringing on a man in David Johnson who was also fresh but who has more experience of our style and understands."

Paisley wins top boss award

Liverpool Echo, April 3, 1982

Bob Paisley added to an impressive list of personal successes today when he was named Bell's Scotch Whisky Manager of the Month for March.

It is the 17th managerial award the Liverpool boss has won and it came during a period in which

... taking the applause of the audience at the end

▶ the Anfield side retained the League Cup with a thrilling 3-1 victory over Spurs at Wembley.

Paisley wins top boss award

Bob Paisley added to an impressive list of personal successes to-day when he was named Bell's Scotch Whisky Manager of the Month for March.

It is the 17th managerial award the Liverpool boss has won and it came during a period in which the Anfield side retained the League

they finally went top with a victory over Notts County.

Mr. Paisley will receive his award, a cheque for £250 and a gallon bottle of Scotch, at Liverpool's next home game.

Jock Wallace, who has guided Leicester to an F.A. Cup semi-final and a healthy

But his award, which follows quickly on the one he picked up in January, as the Reds hit magnificent form after a stuttering start to the season, is as much for his team's surge towards another League Championship.

Victories last month saw them emerge as title favourites and last night they finally went top with a victory over Notts County.

Jock Wallace, who has guided Leicester to an FA Cup semi-final and a healthy League position, has won the Division Two award.

The other half of Bob Paisley's team

**Daily Express
By Lynn Schofield
May 17, 1982**

Not for Bob Paisley a lot of fuss. But he does have one small indulgence.

Beside Jessie stood an array of Bell's Manager of the Month certificates, Manager of the Year and special European Cup award salvers, and in pride of place an OBE citation, which all but cover one wall.

"He is very modest", says Jessie, "but he does like these.

"I told him that at least my award came framed," she joked, pointing to the long service certificate award by Liverpool Education Authority to mark her 25 years in teaching.

"I have to frame all his myself, and it's only with this last one I've found a frame that fits properly. That's why the rest have these funny borders."

Thames Television
Thames Television Limited
306-316 Euston Road
London NW1 3BB
01-387 9494

CONFIDENTIAL

Mrs J Paisley,
c/o 50 Hilary Avenue,
Huyton,
Liverpool.
Merseyside.

7th November 1977

Dear Jessie,

"THIS IS YOUR LIFE"

We are delighted that you will be joining us for the programme on Saturday, 12th November.

I have pleasure in enclosing a first class return rail ticket from Liverpool and should be grateful if you would catch the following train on Friday, 11th November.

Depart Liverpool	Arrive Euston
2.04pm	4.44pm

On your arrival at Euston Station you will be met at the platform barrier by our driver, carrying a small black card reading "THAMES" in white letters. He will take you to The Churchill Hotel, Portman Square, London W.1., where I have reserved accommodation for you at our expense for Friday and Saturday nights. For security reasons, please do not discuss the programme or its content in public places - i.e. hotel, bars or restaurants. I have booked you into the hotel as Mr and Mr B PAVEY, so please sign this name when you check in.

As I mentioned to you on the telephone, there is a script meeting on Friday evening at 7.00pm at Thames Television Studios, Euston Road, and a car will call for you at the hotel at 6.30pm to bring you to this meeting. It will last approximately 1½ hours and the car will return you to the hotel afterwards.

On Saturday morning you will be collected from the hotel at 10.30am and brought to the studios for rehearsal. Would you please bring with you in the morning whatever you intend to wear for the show as there may not be sufficient time for you to return to the hotel between rehearsals and the commencement of the show. At 1.00pm we will break for lunch, which will be provided by us at the studios. After lunch there will be a final rehearsal and then there will be time for you to change and have tea before the programme starts at 6.30pm.

Thames Television
Thames Television Limited
306-316 Euston Road
London NW1 3BB
01-387 9494

Grams Thamestel London NW1
Telex 22816

Registered Address:
306 Euston Road, London NW1 3BB
Registration number 926655
Place of registration: England

Bob Paisley OBE,
14 South Manor Way,
Woolton,
Liverpool L25 9NR.

18 November 1977

My dear Bob

It really was a great pleasure at last being able to throw our happy Book at you. I only hope you enjoyed the experience half as much as we did.

My heartfelt thanks to Jessie for bearing with us so well, and my warmest wishes to you both.

Sincerely,

[signature]

The 'big red book' and letters from Eamonn Andrews and the crew

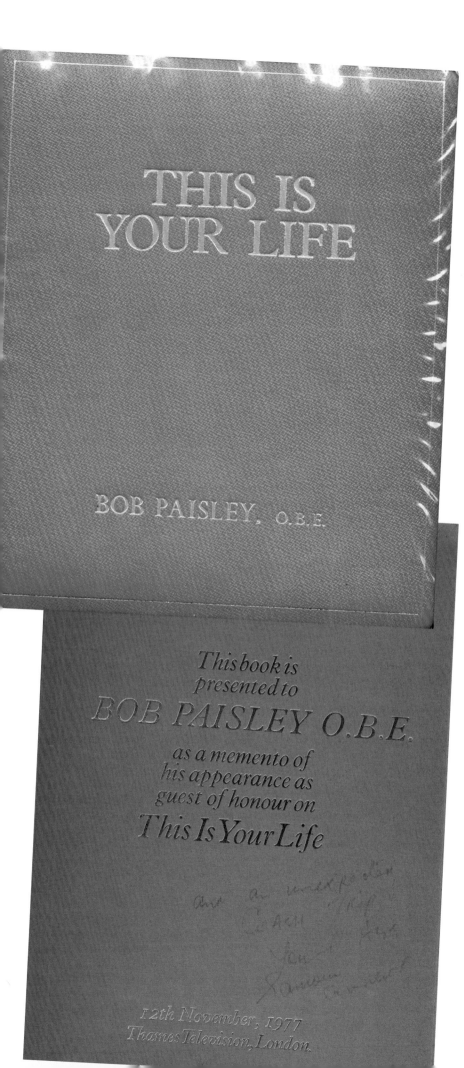

> He met Jessie six years after signing for Liverpool, in April 1939, following an Amateur Cup final triumph with Bishop Auckland.

Her father was not altogether chuffed at the prospect of having a Liverpool footballer for a son-in-law – he supported Manchester United.

Times have changed – Bob Paisley has not.

"It's funny really how this cloth cap image has grown. I suppose I started it," says Jessie.

"You know he's going a bit thin on top?

"Well I told him to get something for his head.

"It's cold sitting in that open directors' box, and he won't wear a trilby or anything like that, so he bought a cap.

"Now he keeps one in a pocket of every coat."

He is still a simple, home-loving family man, according to his wife.

"I once said I came second to football," says Jessie smiling. "But really that's not true. It's his family that comes first.

"I don't think there's anything that he wouldn't do for them he's so devoted.

"Bob loves Sunday afternoons. It's the only time we're together as a family really, and when the grandchildren come in they make straight for their granddad – not me.

"I think it's because he's out so much that he loves his home life. Last week he had five beds in six nights attending away matches and presentation dinners.

"Even in a normal week I never really know what time he'll be in.

"I take him tea and toast in bed in the morning, and he leaves about 8.30 saying 'back at the usual time' but that can be anything.

"I make tea for six, but the hostess tray is handy for keeping his warm.

"Afterwards he just puts his feet up watching television, and often falls asleep.

"Many a time I've ended up just sitting here talking to myself ."

Speaking about Bob's potential retirement plans, Jessie added: "This year, next year, who knows? That bad spell before Christmas got to him. They're not used to bad spells. But I told him you can't go when they're losing. Anyway, he soon got over it.

"When he was ill the other week it was agony. I stayed in the garden out of the way. He lay there, surrounded by the television, radio and phone. Then he came banging on the window, delighted, to say Ian Rush had scored.

"Then he was up again, banging to say Southampton had equalised."

Perhaps fortunately for Jessie, Bob does not bring his work home much. Even on Saturday, hours away from that record 13th championship, he showed no signs of stress.

"As he went out he just said it would be nice to beat them 7-0 like we did three years ago."

Paisley to quit – it's official

Liverpool Echo, August 24, 1982

Bob Paisley is definitely to quit as Liverpool's manager at the end of

Around the piano: The sheet music is for 'Galway Bay'

The budgie who helped Bob to light our fire!

Bob was really settled in the Woolton area of Liverpool where we still live. We have had two houses, 30 years in the present one and 20 in another. Before that, we had a club house in Huyton and paid 25 shillings a week (£1.25p now). It was a lot then but we thought we were lucky.

Bob was never one for pets although we once had a budgie called Pip. That budgie flew free in the room all day and was only put in his cage at night.

When Bob came home at tea-time, there was a fluttering and Pip was out in the hall and on Bob's head!

Also at that time, we had a coke fire, which Bob used to light each morning and kept the box of matches on the mantelpiece.

When Bob was ready, he would call 'matches Pip!' and Pip would knock the matches from the mantelpiece on to the floor with his beak.

If Bob was ever ironing (which he was quite good at doing), Pip always flew on to his shoulder and had to be chased off.

He relaxed in a number of different ways when he was away from Anfield.

He wasn't really what you call a

All smiles: A wedding day picture from the album

this season, it was announced today.

The club ended intense speculation about the future of their manager when chairman Mr John Smith announced officially that Mr Paisley would be stepping down at the end of the season.

Mr Paisley disclosed over the weekend that he had been having talks with the club over his future. The Echo reported yesterday that negotiations were at an advanced stage, that Mr Paisley would also be asked to stay on in a consultative capacity.

Today Mr Smith said: "I wish to announce officially that Mr Paisley no longer desires to be team manager after the end of the coming season.

"However, I am delighted that his association with us will continue in another capacity for years to come.

"The board has the situation under constant review and we hope this statement will clarify the situation before Bob's successor is named at the end of the season."

Front runners to succeed Paisley seem to be John Toshack, now managing Swansea, and Roy Evans, a relatively junior member of the Anfield coaching staff.

True professional

Liverpool Echo comment, August 25, 1982

So Bob Paisley is finally to retire. Not only the many thousands who support Liverpool FC will be sorry to see the departure of this famed figure from the world of professional soccer, but many millions more distant admirers.

But though Paisley has done much to make the team a legend throughout the world and to bring a much-needed focal point of pride for our city, he has done much more.

He has constantly demonstrated to other professional clubs up and down the land the sort of standards they should strive for OFF the pitch as well as on it.

great music lover and never had the radio on in the car, but he enjoyed his Gilbert and Sullivan and also listened to people like Harry Secombe and Jim Reeves.

When it came to TV, Bob was into things like Dad's Army. Of course, he had many stories about his own wartime experiences and there is the famous one when the Liverpool team bus was heading into Rome for the

1977 European Cup Final. Bob said that the last time he was driving down there, he was in a tank.

He never brought his football home with him and would only talk about it if you asked him.

His family life was very important to him and he loved his children and grandchildren. He would have been so proud when the grandchildren gained university degrees.

1982-83

Bob's final season one to remember

Paisley confirmed on August 24, 1982 that this campaign was to be his final one in charge, having first revealed his intentions the previous April.

He told the Liverpool Echo: "If I can judge when the time has come for one of Liverpool's favourite players to move on, then it's only fair that I should be judged by the same standard. It was my decision to step down but it was not easy to make.

"Bill Shankly made the mistake of retiring prematurely and regretted it for the rest of his life. I knew he was wrong and pleaded with him to stay on because I did not want to be manager. I learned from his experience which is why I am sure this is the right time."

The players made sure he went out in style. Having brought in David Hodgson as a replacement for David Johnson, they claimed the First Division title and a third successive League Cup, taking his final tally of honours to 19 in only nine years at the helm.

A 2-1 extra-time victory at Wembley over Manchester United in the latter competition provided Paisley with a poignant moment, as the players insisted their manager go up the famous 39 steps up to the Royal Box first to collect the trophy.

He became the first manager to do so.

The First Division was secured by 11 points, underlining Liverpool's dominance, scoring 87 goals in the process with results including a 5-0 demolition of Everton at Goodison Park. Indeed, this despite the Reds not winning any of their last seven games. Having won the FA Charity Shield against Tottenham, a run of only two defeats in their first 16 games would build the platform for the ensuing success.

Unfortunately a shock 2-1 home defeat to First Division strugglers Brighton in the fifth

round of the FA Cup would end Paisley's hopes of winning the only domestic honour that had eluded him. It was the Reds' first defeat in the FA Cup at Anfield since 1969, and ended an unbeaten home run of 63 matches in all cup competitions since 1974. Widzew Lodz also ended the club's European Cup commitments in the quarter-finals.

There was a clean sweep of player honours for the club. Kenny Dalglish was named Player of the Year by the PFA and the Football Writers, while 21-year-old Ian Rush collected the PFA's Young Player of the Year trophy having established himself as one of the country's top striking talents. Paisley also secured a sixth Bell's Manager of the Year award.

Bruce Grobbelaar, Alan Kennedy and Phil Neal were ever-presents, making 60 appearances while Graeme Souness (59), Sammy Lee (58) and Kenny Dalglish (58) were also prominent. Ian Rush again top-scored with 31 goals from 51 games, while Dalglish netted 20 and defender Neal scored 11 times.

The season had also seen the departure of Terry McDermott, while Waterford-born Jim Beglin would go down as Paisley's final signing, signed for £20,000 from Shamrock Rovers in May 1983 just 10 days into a month's loan.

Paisley throws down the challenge

Liverpool Echo, January 25, 1983

Bob Paisley threw down a challenge last night to bookmakers offering odds of 10-1 against Liverpool making a clean sweep of all major honours open to them this season.

The Anfield manager believes the bookies' figures are "ridiculous" in the light of the fixture congestion Liverpool would face if they continue to

Happy and relaxed on a family break in the Cotswolds in 1964

make progress in the European, FA and Football League Milk Cups while chasing their 14th League Championship.

He declared: "If one of the bookies wants to come and give me £1,000 at those odds, I will give him £10,000 if we win all four and happily pay it with my winning bonuses.

"There is no way the bookies can lose. You only have to look at our fixture list. I have always preached that you take one game at a time, but we have barely got time to do that.

"At critical times there are international weeks with England, Scotland and the Republic of Ireland all involved in fixtures coming up to the Easter programme when we have to play on the Saturday, the Monday and then possibly the Wednesday if we reach the semi-finals of the European Cup.

"People who arrive at these odds have no idea what is involved," Paisley went on. "When you enter competitions you hope to win one.

"There is nothing to stop you trying to win all of them, but the congestion it creates makes it very difficult. If we get replays it will be worse.

"They have stopped taking bets on us for the championship and they are talking about us reaching another Milk Cup final. But we face the prospect of so much football that we could be playing when the milkman comes. And he delivers my milk at five in the morning."

Reds rule and Bob walks alone

Liverpool Daily Post , April 20, 1983

Bob Paisley celebrated alone last night after Everton beat Manchester United at Goodison to secure the League Championship for Liverpool.

An eerie silence had fallen over Anfield as the floodlights glared down on the empty terraces after a reserve match.

Dresden meeting that turned fan into a friend for life

Bob made a surprising friend on one of the club's visits to Dresden in East Germany. His name was Wolfgang Jahnig.

He was a teacher like me. He taught English in a German school and so I suppose that was the link. He went to watch the team train over there and started chatting to Bob.

He then started to correspond with us and was a terrific letter and postcard writer. Dresden were the crack team in East Germany and I think we played them three times in European games.

The relationship developed and Wolfgang even came to Liverpool and stayed with us for a fortnight. Bob laughed because this was the first time Wolfgang had seen bananas.

They didn't have much in East Germany at the time and it was the first time he had been in a supermarket. People must have thought it was strange to see this man having his photo taken standing by the bananas in Sainsbury's.

We also took him to three different local schools so that he could see how they compared with those in Dresden.

He still keeps in touch and writes to us now.

Ein jahrelanger Traum wurde wahr

Unvergeßliche Erlebnisse in der Fußballhochburg Englands

Durfte ich während des Interviews, das ich der Sportredaktion der Union am 20. 6. 1989 gab, von einer Reise zu meinen Freunden nach Liverpool nur träumen, sollte sie im folgenden Jahr Realität werden.

„Freunde durch den Fußball: Wolfgang Jähnig und Bob Paisley", so lautete damals der Titel des Berichts. Nun stand das Wiedersehen mit Bob und das Kennenlernen seiner Familie nach 17 Jahren in der Fußballhochburg Englands unmittelbar bevor.

„Grüße den Bob und übermittle ihm die besten Wünsche", riefen mir zwei Hafenarbeiter nach einem kurzen Gespräch in Dover zu, bevor ich den Zug nach London bestieg. Infolge der Fußballrivalität zwischen dem Südosten und dem Nordwesten Englands eine nicht alltägliche, aber wohltuende Geste dieser beiden Fußballfans.

Was für ein überaus herzlicher Empfang in der Wohnung der Paisleys, an deren Zimmerwänden und in deren Vitrinen die Trophäen der mehrfachen Europa- und League-/Milk-Cup-Erfolge sowie der sechsmaligen Landesmeisterschaft Zeugnis einer tollen Erfolgskette

WOLFGANG JÄHNIG hält den „Charity Shield" und den „Football Association Cup" in den Armen, den die Reds 1989/90 gewannen.

A dream lasting for years became true

Unforgettable highlights in the football stronghold of England

During the interview on June 20 in 1989 I was still dreaming of a visit to my friends in Liverpool, before it became reality in the following year.

"Friends through football, Wolfgang Jähnig and Bob Paisley" was the headline of the newspaper report at that time. Suddenly the reunion with Bob and making the aquaintance with his family in the football stronghold of England was imminent.

"Greet Bob and give him our best wishes", two dockers had shouted to me after a short talk in Dover, before I got in the train to London. In spite of the football rivalry between the Southeast and the Northwest of England a not daily but pleasant gesture of the two football fans.

What a heartfelt welcome in the home of the Paisleys on whose walls and in whose sideboards the trophies of numerous European, League and Milk Cup successes as well as the sixfold League Championships demonstrate the great management of Bob Paisley from 1974 to 1983, who was awarded with the O.B.E. in Buckingham Palace by Queen Elizabeth II. in 1977.

I'm still impressed by the great hospitality at Anfield Road, the Reds' homeground. Welcomed in the programme and through the loudspeaker as the red-hot fan before the English Cup tie between F. C. Liverpool and F. C. Southampton, that all had an emotional effect on me, a seat in the "Director's Box" completed the marks of honour on that unforgettable day. I also got to know the traditional rooms, which are carpeted in red. In the souvenir shop I could choose according to my desire.

During my two-week-stayBob's wife Jessie and her sons surprised me day by day. I enjoyed the welcome at the townhall in Liverpool and the visit to the Anglican and Metropolitan Cathedrals, which are so different from each other. My thoughts went back some decades, when I stood in front of the statues of the Beatles in "Cavern Walks", where they started their carrier. By visiting English families and three schools I could make use of the English language, too.

I don't want to forget my football friends and support F. C. Everton, the Parr family, whom I have ...
"Goodison Park". The Cup ti...
ham Athletic mean...

Wolfgang Jähnig's special pride: The original kits of the two Liverpool Clubs

---

Eine reich belohnte Überwindung

Freunde durch den Fußball: Wolfgang Jähnig und Bob Paisley

A richly rewarded effort

Friends through football - Wolfgang Jähnig and Bob Paisley

Souvenir collectors are no rarity in our country. Also the principle to pay visit to a great athlete, to snatch an autograph, a badge or something like that, to say »thanks« - it's always the same. Always? all right, almost always. There's an example whose development almost sounds like a tale. Let's do it in succession.

Once upon a time there was ... in March 1973. The quarter final of the UEFA-Cup competition between Dynamo Dresden and F.C. Liverpool took place. The team with world-wide reputation took lodgings at the "Interhotel Newa". At the entrance souvenir hunters were pushing among them a man in the prime of life who had other aims. He wanted to speak English to a regular Englishman. Any goes without saying. For professional reasons, that how he succeeded in getting into the hotel. He was looking round to catch foreign voices. He took his heart and turned to an official of the Liverpool delegation. So a friendship began that has been lasting till today – the friendship between the Dresden teacher Wolfgang Jähnig and the ex-manager of L.F.C., Bob Paisley.

Today wolfgang jähnig about the first meeting with the father of Liverpool's successful time in the seventies: "I made him for my profession and soon we were on the same wave-length, for Bob's wife is a teacher, too. There was not much time for long talks, but this quarter of an hour was solitary, because all who were sitting round the table, primarily Bob Paisley, were so kind and interested. Last but not least I got diverse souvenirs. Was that an event."

Bound in gratitude Wolfgang sent a smoking gang to the manager's family. It contributed to a permanent contact in the English language, to play game between the two teams followed in 1976. There was a little bit more time to talk to Bob and the staff from the Isle. When a year later the lot brought Liverpool and Dynamo together for the ...

In his office below the Main Stand the Reds' boss toasted success quietly with a glass of whisky.

Although the trophy became Liverpool's in their absence, a delighted Mr Paisley said: "I didn't mind when we won it."

Without Everton's success the Reds would have had to win at home next Saturday against Norwich.

"The earlier the better. Obviously it saves us sweating more than we should against Norwich on Saturday," he said relaxing in his modest office.

"There was no point in my going to watch Everton and United. We have finished with them this season. But we did hope Everton would win.

"We like to win things ourselves but I think we have won the championship ourselves by consistency," the Reds' boss said. "It's been a team effort and not down to me."

Reds rule and Bob walks alone

With an eye to the future he added: "Next year, if Liverpool triumph again, I hope to associate with that type of thing and help someone to achieve it."

Earlier...(he) had watched Liverpool reserves come from 2-0 down to win 3-2.

In a smart camel coat and cap Mr Paisley had sat inscrutably throughout the game as the championship issue was being settled just across Stanley Park.

He was asked if he had thought of the Everton match during the evening: "Never crossed my mind," came the terse reply.

"No way could I go to Goodison. No way could I get pleasure out of it."

And with unswerving dedication despite his imminent stepdown as manager, he added: "Tonight's biggest concern was looking to see what we've got to win the championship with next season.

"Now we've got to finish the season and give our supporters value for money," he added before leaving quietly for home.

In the Commons last night Liverpool's Labour MPs tabled a motion putting on record: "Congratulations to Liverpool Football Club on its magnificent achievement in winning the First Division championship for the 14th time."

The motion also congratulated the club for winning this year's Milk Cup and wished Bob Paisley "a long and happy retirement from the game he has adorned for nearly half a century."

My secret title fear – Paisley

**Liverpool Echo
April 20, 1983**

"After the way we came through to take the title last season, I knew we had the players to win it again but there was always the danger that injuries might throw us out of our stride," said Paisley.

"With all the matches we have to play, in domestic competitions and in Europe, you really need a squad of about 16 players and some of the German clubs have as many as 18.

"We have had to manage with about 14 and that leaves you vulnerable if you suffer injuries in certain positions.

"It was that sort of consideration that made me buy Mark Lawrenson at the start of last season because he is very adaptable as well as very consistent.

"Phil Neal, Kenny Dalglish and Craig Johnston have also proved they can play in two or three positions and that has helped us a lot. Phil and Kenny are both in their 30s but they are very fit and very knowledgeable.

"I have always said that you can't judge age by the calendar because there are certain players who are so well adjusted mentally that they can pace themselves without affecting their game.

I remember when illness first struck – Bob was driving and didn't know the way home

Together: Enjoying an open topped bus ride

> "On the whole I think it has
been a good season. At the start,
quite a lot of teams seemed
willing to come out and play
against us but later on we found
people tightened up if they
became involved in relegation
trouble, which is understandable.

"We have had some fine games
and I hope we have some more
before the end of the season,
because our players will be
relaxed and comfortable now and
looking forward to entertaining
the crowds.

"The best clubs have come at
us and helped to make their
matches good ones. It is usually
the weaker sides, who are
worried about losing and play
tight, that causes us the biggest
problems."

Bob reveals secrets of his 'marathon men'

Liverpool Daily Post, April 21, 1983

"I have always preferred to liken
the championship to a marathon.
You have to know how to start the
race, how to take the strain when
problems come along and to
make sure you don't give any
potentially dangerous rivals an
advantage," Paisley revealed.

"My policy is to ideally have five
or six men around the age of 26,
a couple of youngsters, a couple
around the 28 mark and one or
two in their 30s.

"But the nucleus of the team
should be experienced and not
too old. You don't just look at the
calendar.

"The medical side is an
important yardstick. Our two over
30s are Phil Neal and Kenny
Dalglish.

"Phil is the type of player who
does not often get injured. Kenny
takes more knocks than the
others, but he is very strong.

"They have been outstanding
from a stamina point of view as
well as in skill.

"They have kept going as well
as anyone. But they still need that
help from the younger players."

Whenever Bob went away
for a European game he
always brought me back
a plaque with the name of the town
or city.

I've still got them all. Sometimes
he would bring me back a blouse to
wear and so he was obviously
thinking about us when he was away.
He would also bring back a doll in
national costume for our daughter
Christine.

Eventually we had to face up to the
fact in retirement that Bob was
starting to become unwell.

When he finally went into the
Nursing Home, that was the worst

time for me. It was just as bad as
when he died. He had reached the
stage when he couldn't understand
things.

I remember the first time that
happened. We were coming home
from the Liverpool football ground
and reached the top of our road.

Bob turned to me and said: 'Where
do we go now?' I said: 'Don't be
daft, Bob. You know we live down
here!' The truth was, he didn't know.

He would go each Sunday to visit
Robert and his wife Irene and take
fruit for them. One day he forget
where he lived. He didn't know
where the house was.

> **Paisley's lesson**
> **April 21, 1983**

Liverpool Daily Post Editorial

At a time when the Merseyside Chamber of Commerce has produced an economic survey of a profoundly mournful nature, spraying yet more gloom around the region, it is appropriate to pay tribute to a man who in recent years has done more for the morale of Merseyside than any other. We raise our caps to Mr Bob Paisley.

Mr Paisley has nothing whatsoever to do with the daily frustrations of producing goods, which are increasingly difficult to sell in hardening markets. He faces none of the tough challenges of competing in cut-throat export wars. The battle he has fought and in which he has succeeded brilliantly has been possibly even more important.

He has given to this region, which has probably taken more hard knocks than any other in Britain, a fierce and unquenchable pride which has survived even the worst days of economic adversity. Liverpool Football Club has kept a flag flying high.

Mr Paisley, a modest man in a fraternity not noted for humility, will say that the credit for Liverpool's latest major achievement must be shared. That is true but as a growing number of sacked football bosses would agree it is the manager who shoulders the real burden. In the hour of his greatest triumph supported by the proposal to make him a freeman of the city, none would deny him the lion's share of the praise.

My first game — and a lucky charm from abroad that gave me a fright

The programme from Jessie's first football game – an FA Cup first leg tie at Bolton in 1946 which Liverpool lost 5-0! Left: Bob's lucky troll!

There are lots of things I have kept that remind me of our time together. I have kept a programme from the first football game I went to see Bob in. We also have the original lucky troll that Bob brought back from Denmark.

I'll never forget when I first saw it. I woke up one morning and went down to the kitchen. I just saw two eyes looking up at me from the kitchen floor. I wondered what it was.

It was a lucky charm for him and he kept it during his time as manager. There's a horse shoe wrapped around his waist. I don't know where that came from but it's been on there for years, it must have been put on for luck. There's one in the Liverpool museum but this is the original one. Bob kept it for years.

Celebrating a nursing home anniversary in 1993. Below: A photo from the garden

'I'LL NEVER FORGET WHEN I FIRST SAW IT. I WOKE UP ONE MORNING AND WENT DOWN TO THE KITCHEN. I JUST SAW TWO EYES LOOKING UP AT ME FROM THE KITCHEN FLOOR. IT WAS A LUCKY CHARM FOR HIM'

The world of sport is passing through troubled times. Endless rows over involvements with South Africa, mark the converging courses of sport and politics. Many will regret that this should be so. It is however, an indication of the increasingly influential part that sport plays in our lives.

Today, Liverpool are deservedly the champions, the envy of every football-kicking kid from one end of the country to the other. We ARE the greatest, so why shouldn't we shout about it? Today it's football.

Who knows, someday it may be industry.

Paisley blasts fixture farce

Liverpool Echo
April 28, 1983

"The situation is farcical at the moment. You have players away with their countries and you don't see them again until a few hours before the match," said Paisley.

"It is reported that Ronnie Whelan was injured playing for Ireland yesterday, but I won't see him or Mark Lawrenson until tomorrow morning, shortly before we have to set out for Tottenham.

"Ian Rush was playing his first match for three weeks for Wales, even though he wasn't match fit, and he came off half an hour from the end.

"He took one terrible foul and I won't know until later today whether or not he'll be able to play on Saturday.

"People talk about needing all the fixtures, but the present situation is crippling.

"League soccer is our livelihood and it shouldn't have to suffer in this way.

"International football is vitally important too, because it affects the whole of our national game.

"Somewhere along the line people have to sit down and plan the two properly, so that both the clubs and the international sides get a fair crack of the whip."

Team of all the talents

Cup that Cheers... proud manager Bob Paisley and his richer section-leading championship team

An emotional Bob
pays tribute to fans

Time for reflection

DAILY POST SPORT

Just champion!

'It was a very emotional experience. It hasn't fully dawned on me yet that this was my last game. It will hit me when I realise I can't go in the dressing room any more.'

More pictures and stories — Pages 26,27

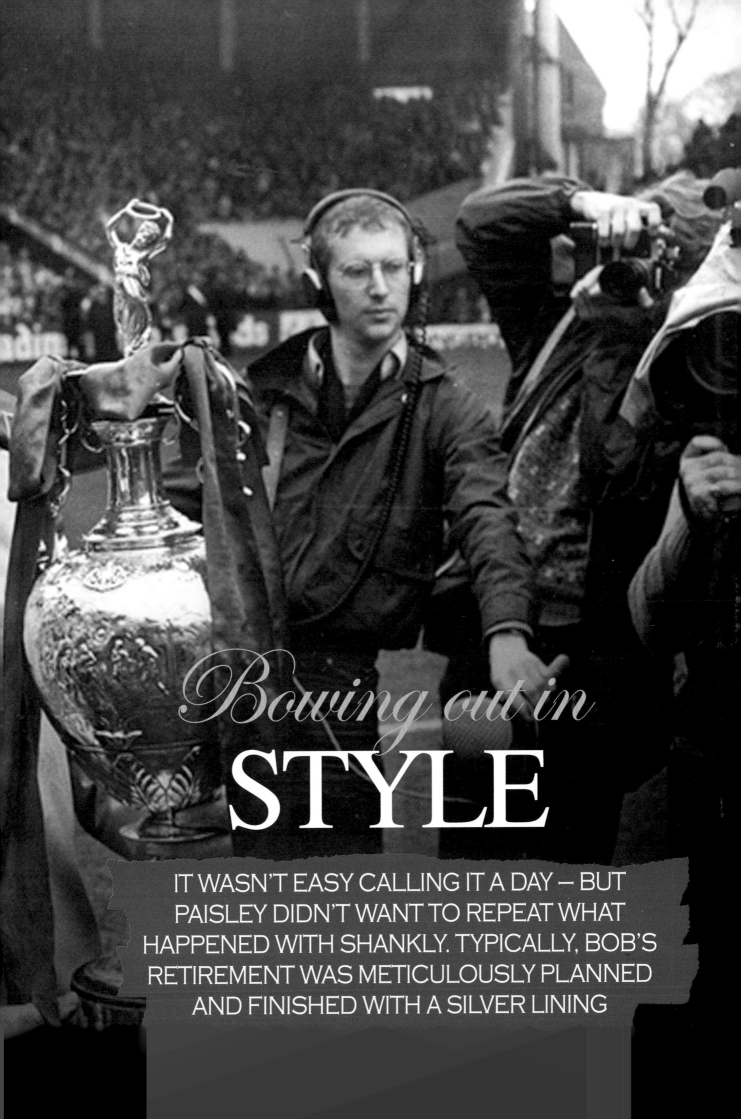

Bowing out in STYLE

IT WASN'T EASY CALLING IT A DAY — BUT PAISLEY DIDN'T WANT TO REPEAT WHAT HAPPENED WITH SHANKLY. TYPICALLY, BOB'S RETIREMENT WAS METICULOUSLY PLANNED AND FINISHED WITH A SILVER LINING

Liverpool Echo, 1983

My Life

After he called it a day, Bob Paisley revealed his thoughts on a whole range of issues to the Liverpool Echo in a special series called 'My Life'. This and other articles in the spring of 1983 reveal his motives for quitting and his feelings about a fond Wembley farewell

First match could have seen my downfall

There were problems in the first match (pre-season in August 1974) against Kaiserslautern. One of the German players went in dangerously on Ray Kennedy and several of our lads reacted angrily, with the result that the referee gave Kevin Keegan his marching orders.

I had to think quickly. If the sending-off was reported to the FA in London, then Kevin could have faced a suspension, which was something I obviously wanted to avoid. So I told Peter Cormack that he had been the culprit, not Kevin, and pleaded a case of mistaken identity. We stuck so firmly to the story that we even had Kevin and Peter believing it! As it happened, our efforts were not really necessary because the referee could not attend the London hearing of the case and the matter was dropped.

Football and Liverpool have been my life – a drug I've been hooked on

I reached my decision…as a new generation of Anfield players were sweeping towards the 1982 championship and League Cup double.

The time had come and two thoughts were uppermost in my mind. The first was that young players had broken through into the team to provide a foundation to pass on to my successor.

The second was that I had become aware of growing speculation amongst our fans and the general public about when I was going to retire. That can only have an unsettling effect, and you cannot ignore it. They were starting to ask similar questions before Bill Shankly dropped the bombshell of his retirement and it is frustrating for both parties – me and the fans.

So I came to the conclusion that it was time for a new manager, and I envisaged my successor being one of these three: Joe Fagan, Ronnie Moran or Roy Evans.

The club has to give one of them a chance, because who is to say who will make a manager or who won't?

Who was to say whether I would succeed when I followed Bill in 1974? At the same time, Liverpool have expressed a keenness for me to stay on in some form of advisory capacity – which could be difficult.

The business of offering advice is fraught with problems. It would never have worked, for instance, if Bill had stayed in that capacity when I took over from him. Bill didn't give advice. He gave orders. But advice, by its very nature, must be something other people can take or leave.

Whatever happens, leaving the manager's chair at Anfield is going to be a massive wrench for me. Football and Liverpool have been my life, a drug I've been hooked on.

My prime consideration when I was mulling over the prospect of retirement was the team my successor would inherit. The way youngsters like Ronnie Whelan and Ian Rush have come through, helping to win two trophies in their first season at the top level, has influenced me greatly.

> '**I HAD BECOME AWARE OF GROWING SPECULATION AMONGST OUR FANS AND THE GENERAL PUBLIC ABOUT WHEN I WAS GOING TO RETIRE. THAT CAN ONLY HAVE AN UNSETTLING EFFECT AND YOU CANNOT IGNORE IT'**

Silver service resumed: Celebrating his sixth and final title triumph

Return of the Gladiator

The only sober men in Rome (after Liverpool had won the European Cup for the first time in 1977) that night were me, the Pope and Horace Yates, teetotal sports editor of the Liverpool Daily Post.

Yet five days earlier, when the players trooped off at Wembley with their heads down after losing to Manchester United, a victory over Borussia Moenchengladbach seemed a million miles away.

We travelled straight home from Wembley with the players depressed, and it was then that fate stepped in to help us.

One of the special trains ahead of us on our way back to Liverpool broke down, and we were stuck for almost two hours.

Of course there was alcohol on the train, and the players were drinking – not to excess, but to help drown the disappointment.

In that state of mind you don't need much, and that extra couple of hours on the train was all they needed to switch from depression to defiance.

By the time we reached Lime Street they were ready to take on the Germans there and then.

Top professional footballers are like thoroughbred racehorses, they are highly strung and susceptible to atmosphere.

If their heads had stayed down there was no way they could have won in Rome, and if that train had been on time they would probably have gone home in the wrong frame of mind.

So we travelled to Rome in exactly the right mood.

Super Kev was a key man in Rome

One man stood out in particular, for he used that final in Rome to play his finest game for Liverpool in his last match for the club – Kevin Keegan.

By then he was more or less transferred to Hamburg, but his performance that night proved he was worth every mark the Germans had agreed to pay.

Kevin had a wanderlust, and he played really well in only about half-a-dozen games for Liverpool that season because of his frustration and his desire to move on.

In turn the crowd became frustrated with him and I'm sure if he had turned in a performance against Manchester United like the one he gave against Borussia, then we would have won the FA Cup.

How my dreams nearly ended

Like other working-class lads in the North East, I naturally turned to football, not just as a recreation, but as a way of life.

I was lucky because my school, Eppleton Senior Mixed, was years ahead of its time as far as football was concerned.

The school caretaker, Bowler Burns, would give mustard baths in the boiler house, while the sports masters, Bertie Rowe, Jimmy Johnson and Alec Wright, supervised the running and organisation of the team.

Sing on . . . where's the extra verse?

I know at Anfield the reputation of the Kop has varying effects on referees. They are only human, and like the rest of us, have different personalities.

Some will be intimidated and give a majority of the 50-50 decisions in Liverpool's favour, while others will take a defiant stance and, in effect, tell the Kop to go to hell by giving those decisions the other way.

But even those great fans on the Kop couldn't please Bill Shankly all of the time. I remember once Bill being quite upset one match that they had stopped singing You'll Never Walk Alone too soon.

'They should have given us another verse,' Bill said to me – and he wasn't joking either!

The Player Of The Seventies?

Ray (Kennedy) had lost his appetite for playing up front, but I learned he was in midfield as a schoolboy. He was surprised I'd found that out.

A TRIBUTE TO
BOB PAISLEY

SPONSORED BY K.P. FOODS LIMITED

This special dinner has been organised to pay tribute to the most successful football manager in history – Mr. Bob Paisley – who retires today from a glittering career with Liverpool Football Club which in total has spanned over 44 years.

Funds raised this evening, will go to the Merseyside Grand National Aintree Campaign which, as you will all know, has recently managed to save the Grand National from extinction.

HOLIDAY INN HOTEL, LIVERPOOL.
8.00 p.m. – MAY 23rd 1983

We were there.
We saw Bob Paisley's Liverpool team playing. When wide-eyed grand-children ask in years to come, we'll tell them of Dalglish and Souness and the days when Liverpool really had a side.

We won't exaggerate.
We won't have to.
We saw those three European Cup triumphs, those epic Wembley finals, those six titles in eight years – yes, and the First Division was a hard league to win in those days.

We were there.
We saw Bob Paisley's team making history. And when his name is mentioned, some of the happiest and most exciting memories of our lives will come flooding back, and we'll tell them about the Greatest.

Emotion of going up to lift Cup got to me

Liverpool Daily Post, March 28, 1983

Not only did the Reds break new ground by winning the League Cup for the third successive season – Paisley became the first manager to mount the Wembley steps and collect a trophy.

Liverpool defeated their rivals Manchester United 2-1 after extra time and the victorious captain Graeme Souness handed over the ultimate honour to his boss.

Paisley, making his 12th and last Wembley appearance before retiring at the end of the season, was forced to overcome his early reluctance.

"I didn't want to do it at first. But then I realised what a magnificent gesture it was on the players' part and I couldn't refuse then," he said.

"I've been to Wembley many times now but I've never been up those steps before and I must admit the emotion got to me when I did."

Said skipper Graeme Souness: "It was purely spontaneous. We wanted him to go up because it was his last year, and he deserves the credit as much as any of the players. I wanted him to take my place."

Paisley said the final was "the hardest game I've ever had." and went on to sharply criticise the heavy Wembley surface: "That pitch is on the way out. It's got to come up. It was strength-sapping. It killed Spurs that way last year and did the same to United. Nerves can do that to players as well in a final, but I have never seen so many men go down in one team."

But that knowledge turned out to be a blessing for both Ray and the club. I had a talk with him and told him we'd try him out in midfield in the reserves. The result exceeded our wildest expectations.

Ray blossomed in the role, made a first-team place his own and went on to play for England. When he signed for Liverpool the £200,000 fee was then a club record – but he proved one of the greatest investments Liverpool ever made.

His contribution to Liverpool's achievements was enormous and his consistency remarkable. So much so, in fact, that on the rare occasions he missed a match, his absence was felt deeply, simply because he was a midfield powerhouse with tremendous vision and knowledge of the game.

He showed the ability to open up a game and give you the width of the park. When intercepting a loose ball invariably he would hit a telling pass – and running on to one himself he was as good as anyone I've seen.

He was many people's choice as English football's player of the seventies.

Ray, in my view, was one of Liverpool's greatest players and probably the most underrated and he was totally mis-used at England level.

We know what his strengths were at Liverpool, things were built around him and we played according to his abilities, which were recognised throughout Europe – except in England. He never received the acclaim he deserved in this country. I wished I still had him around.

Why I sold the country's best keeper

The unique demands made on a Liverpool player were a major factor in Ray Clemence's decision to ask for a move after 14 years at Anfield.

Sometimes players don't realise the pressure they are under – and Ray was under plenty when he was at Liverpool. Apart from the challenge of constantly trying to win things with the club,

❯ he had the rivalry for the England job of Peter Shilton and the limelight trained on him because of his regular appearances on radio and television.

Then our signing of Bruce Grobbelaar from Vancouver Whitecaps was probably the last straw that pushed Ray to ask for a move. My plan was the tried and trusted one at Liverpool of grooming Bruce in the reserves for a couple of years as a gradual successor to Ray.

But Bruce, never short of confidence, told Ray that he'd have his place before the end of the season. It meant that Ray faced a battle he had never faced in his life before that. He came to me and said: "Who does this fellow think he is?"

Finally he came to see me and said he wanted a transfer. It was granted – and at a bargain price – simply because of all that he'd done for the club. But for his great service the fee would not have been a penny under £450,000 rather than the £300,000 Keith Burkinshaw paid to take him to Tottenham. It was washers for the best goalkeeper in the country who, even though he's well into his thirties, is fit enough to go on playing until he's 40.

Show TV pundit Jimmy over the Hill

I think it wrong that someone with a vested interest should also be in a powerful position to sway the opinions of millions of people on television every weekend.

Jimmy Hill has access to millions of soccer fans on Match of the Day – considerably more than actually attend matches.

And in that capacity he has been guilty of several misguided comments concerning my club.

What he says about others is for them to comment on but I won't be silent when I hear someone like Jimmy Hill informing the nation of where we have gone wrong, which was the case after our European Cup defeat in Tbilisi in 1979.

I had to show who was boss – but I didn't drive Bill away from Anfield

I took over from Bill knowing that even if we had any success I would not get the credit for it.

People have said that I drove Bill away from the club.

The relationship certainly became uneasy for a while and in the eyes of many I was the villain of the piece.

But just as Bill had said on the day he arrived from Huddersfield 15 years earlier – "I'm the boss now and we'll do it my way" – so I had to say the same thing.

There was no way that I would have driven Bill away from Liverpool.

I didn't want his job.

I even tried talking him into staying, and suggested that if he went away on a world cruise to recharge his batteries we could see if we could handle it together when he came back.

But Bill just said that he'd had enough, and that was that.

I had one object in mind and that was to stabilise the position.

At first, after he finished, he would come down to our training ground at Melwood. The players still called him 'Boss,' and it didn't bother me. I both expected and accepted it.

Then there was a report in a Sunday paper after a game at Ipswich quoting me as saying that even in Bill's day I used to run the show. It was totally untrue but Bill took offence. I apologised. He was still free to come down to the training ground, but it was his decision not to come down any more. In the end he acknowledged that it had been the right thing.

I didn't ask him for advice – even though I could have done with some – because he had had enough of management.

Anyway, after 15 years working with the man I knew that Bill wouldn't give advice – he would issue orders.

BOB PAISLEY

A LIVERPOOL ECHO TRIBUTE

WHEN BOB CALLED IT A DAY, THE LIVERPOOL
ECHO PRODUCED A SPECIAL BOOK AS A
TRIBUTE TO HIS ACHIEVEMENTS

There are only two copies of Bob Paisley: A Liverpool Echo Tribute. One was presented to the Liverpool manager by the Echo's Head of Sport Vincent Kelly (above) and the other is still retained by the newspaper. The leather-backed book was published to coincide with his retirement in 1983, and contained tributes from famous names along with never-seen-before photos from the Paisley photo album

He did not need to rant and rave

In those early years his advice was invaluable to all who worked with him. He did not need to rant and rave to make his point. Bob Paisley demonstrated that a calm, calculated brain, good common sense and no 'fancy dan' ideas can achieve the ultimate success

Gordon Milne

His character as reliable as his tackling

As a friend and former playing colleague, I've known Bob Paisley for 35 years. In that time, I've come to value him as a man whose character off the field is as staunch and reliable as his tackling was on it.

His deep knowledge of football has made him the greatest manager in the game today. Hand in hand with his soccer knowledge goes a tremendous sense of humour which he had as a player and is still with him – how else could he have coped with those sports journalists who have plagued his life for so long, including myself?

I know I am only one among many who deeply regret Bob's decision to 'call it a day' after over 40 years' association with Anfield.

Albert Stubbins

An old master who could teach me the game

My first match at Anfield was at right half-back for Aston Villa back in the fifties. The roar from the Kop was awesome as Billy Liddell waltzed down the left wing, making us look like idiots.

Then I began to recognise the source of Liddell's magic. He was Liverpool's ageing, inconspicuous craftsman at left-half – Bob Paisley. Bob's play was smart and experienced; its smooth, simple style hiding its effectiveness. Here was another old master who could teach me the game just by watching his moves.

Danny Blanchflower

He lets his players do the talking

Bob Paisley is the most modest and successful manager in the history of the English First Division since Herbert Chapman. Bob's low profile type of management is so very different from the average modern managers; he lets the players' performance do the talking and keeps on picking up Cups and Championships.

Joe Mercer

Like Shanks, Bob was competitive

We met at Anfield in the 1938/39 season but the war separated us and it was 1946 before we played together regularly in the first team. We had a great understanding when I was on the left wing and Bob was left half, and I owe a lot to him for the service he gave me.

Service and devotion are the qualities that Bob has given to Liverpool and I have no hesitation in saying that he is the best servant that the Reds have ever had. Player, trainer, coach, physiotherapist, assistant manager and manager, a success in every position and, without question, the most successful manager that football has known.

We had one or two good tricks worked out that often caught defences napping. Bob had a tremendous throw and sometimes I would feint to go down the wing, and he would throw the ball across my body, so that when I straightened up and cut inside it fell nicely for me.

If Paisley threw the ball over my head I knew there was nobody behind me and I could put my head down and go straight for goal.

Like Shankly, Bob was a great competitor.

Billy Liddell

His obsession was success for Liverpool

In my long years of contact with Liverpool FC, initially with Bill Shankly as manager, I have always found Bob Paisley with one thing on his mind – his obsession for success at his club.

It was obvious to everyone that he played an important part alongside Bill in building Liverpool's great reputation at home and in Europe.

When he took charge of the club it came as no surprise to me, as the men in charge knew Bob's influence was sure to keep the team on the successful vein they were accustomed to. His tremendous success has always been accepted in the usual Paisley manner. Not bombastic, no room for self-praise, but with appreciation to all around him – and especially the players.

He was set a difficult task to follow one of the game's great managers. He upheld the tradition and improved on these feats.

Jock Stein

His achievements are good for the city

Bob Paisley is the kind of manager every club would like to have. He gets on with the job, has a reputation for integrity and modesty second to none – and he gets results! Of course I would like Everton to have the sort of record Liverpool have had under Bob. But if we cannot achieve that excellence yet, there is no better place for it than at Anfield.

Liverpool's outstanding success has been good for the city, good for the country and good for football. Bob's part in it cannot be overstated.

Sir John Moores

He is on the same level as Sinatra in his field

There is no magic formula, there is no mystery about Anfield, it's just down to pure talent. Bob Paisley epitomises that and I am amazed that people in football, who ought to know better, do not just accept the fact.

He is on the same level as Sinatra in his field and nobody should question his talent. It's not the fact that he's got a bigger band or sings on bigger stages, it's just down to ability.

The man oozes talent and he talks more common sense than ten of us other managers put together – he probably works harder than ten of us put together as well!

Brian Clough

He never knew when he was beaten

Bob Paisley is the most modest and successful manager in the history of the English First Division since Herbert Chapman.

For the benefit of the younger football fans, he was the man who was manager of Huddersfield Town in the middle-1920s, who won three consecutive First Division championships in a row, then went to Arsenal and did it again.

Bob's low profile type of management is so very different from the average modern managers; he lets the players' performance do the talking and keeps on picking up Cups and Championships.

In his playing days at Liverpool, he was a wing half (as we called them in those days) and played in a non-stop uncomplicated way. Hard, tough and fair in the tackle and never knew when he was beaten.

I obviously wish him a happy retirement but, knowing Bob, I don't believe it.

Joe Mercer

He gave nothing less than everything

I am sure that I am speaking for all the members of the supporters' club – and indeed all fans – when I say that Bob Paisley has given us nothing but 100 per cent effort in every role, as player, coach and manager.

Although Bob has brought home more trophies and honours than any other person in the game, he still remains the most modest, down-to-earth man.

Long may he be associated with our great club.

Ted Black, Chairman, LFC Supporters Club

He's like a bear with a sore head when we lose

He tells the lads to keep a level head when we are winning but he is like a bear with a sore head when we lose – and that makes him more determined to win the next match.

Joe Fagan

He kept a low profile – especially before a derby!

The job at Everton was a very big one, particularly when Liverpool were so strong. I was always mindful of keeping a low profile, especially when it came to the derbies. I was conscious that Bob wouldn't say too much before these games, which was the right thing to do.

Gordon Lee

Players needed to fit in to the system

It is said that he plays a simple game yet nobody has been able to match his consistency. Great players are needed to fit into the system and, no matter what they cost, they still have to serve an Anfield apprenticeship. Competition is so fierce for places that players must produce consistently good performances to stay in the side.

Howard Kendall

Bob could be a practical joker!

He appears to be a quiet man on the surface, yet everyone at Anfield knows that he has got a keen sense of humour and still plays quite a few tricks. I can remember him putting on a trilby and coming to the outside office window to ask for tickets in a very broad accent. They didn't recognise him until he burst out laughing! That's Bob – a likeable man who has won more honours in the game than any other manager.

Peter Robinson

A loyal and hard working manager

Our success during the past 20 years can be attributed to the complete dedication of all our staff, including our two famous managers. Service to the club is uppermost in the minds of everyone, from the directors down.

I have no doubt that our success on the field is due to what happens off the field. In paying my tribute to Bob I would like to say I do not know a chairman of any other British club who has had such a loyal and hard-working manager.

John Smith

By 2.45pm he paced up and down – more nervous than the players

He was actually a guy who wore his emotions on his sleeve. By 2.45pm, you could tell what he was going through just by looking at his face. He would be pacing up and down and taking sips of water. He looked more nervous than the players, although I think he did his best to try not to show it.

He was a real father figure to me. He was a good guy, someone you could go to with your problems. He was different to Bill Shankly in so many ways. If you were larking about in the corridors and Shanks came along, you shut up. But Bob was very much more easy-going, a friendlier type of guy.

I went through a particularly bad time after a cartilage operation and I remember Bob pulling me to one side after I'd had a bloody awful game and saying: 'Give it time. I know you're giving 100 per cent. Don't worry. It will come.' He could lose his temper and have a go at people, but that would always be behind closed doors. The players appreciated that. Everyone knows he didn't want the job. But I don't think he ever came to terms with it – even after all the success he had. He did have quite a sense of humour, but he was a very uncomplicated guy and a little bit of an introvert.

Ian Callaghan

Success has not changed him

To follow Bill Shankly at Anfield would not have been just an ordeal but perhaps an impossibility. When everyone in football measures Bob Paisley's achievements since Bill Shankly's retirement, it is without doubt the most breathtaking and commendable record in the history of football in our country.

While all of that is remarkable, for me, the most wonderful part of it all is that Bob Paisley is still just Bob. He is the same likeable, honest, solid, uncomplicated and unchangeable man since the day any of us got to know him.

Bobby Robson

'You've taken all my whisky!'

I remember Bob coming to watch a game at United soon after he had announced his intention to retire. He came into my office after the match, looking so relaxed. When I asked him if he would like a drink, he replied: "I would like a whisky but it doesn't look as though you have any Bell's." I replied: "I haven't – you've taken it all for the past seven years!"

Ron Atkinson

Shrewd buying

I first met Bob Paisley during our Championship year of 1946-47. He showed tremendous zest for the game and was a type of player you would always have in your team. Recent years have shown very shrewd buying and the knowledge that those players would knit together to form the most outstanding club side in the history of the game.

Phil Taylor

We all wanted to play for him

If I could win a quarter of what Bob Paisley won then I would consider myself very, very successful.

For someone who didn't want the job, he didn't do too badly, did he? His record is incredible and will never be beaten. He had absolutely no problem getting the players to play for him and understand exactly what he wanted. That was just one of Bob's gifts which is often underestimated. He had so much humility.

Kevin Keegan

We held him in great affection

He had this habit when he was talking to us before a big game of pointing to a drawer in his office and saying: 'If we win this one, I've got things in there you won't believe!'

But we weren't in it for the money. There was a special bond between the players and between the players and the manager and coaching staff. We all held Bob Paisley in great affection.

David Fairclough

Sound advice

Bob is second to none when it comes to assessing the strengths and weaknesses of players and his vast knowledge of the game and how it should be played is reflected in his vast personal list of achievements during the last decade.

Although I have only been in management (at Swansea) a relatively short time, I have been grateful on more than one occasion for his sound advice and must admit to having been influenced by him tremendously.

John Toshack

'Hey Joey, sit down – you'll start another civil war!'

I owe Bob Paisley a great deal and it was indeed an honour for me to be his first signing. I've tried to listen and learn from the 'wise old owl' and I hope that I have been a credit to him.

Going into Europe with Bob reminded me of the reverse of Julius Caesar coming over to conquer this country. It was like taking your army all over Europe knowing that you were invincible. That was how Bob made you feel. He gave us the confidence as a unit to say it doesn't matter if it's -11C in Wroclaw – we can achieve. It was lovely to be alongside him and not just for the success, because the atmosphere he created was great.

He was a very warm and funny man too. The humour maybe didn't come through all the time in public but he did make us laugh. Even in the lead-ups to big finals he would be throwing little one-liners in here and there to relax us all. We went to Barcelona in the 1975-76 UEFA Cup semi-final where they were unbeaten and we won 1-0. Just before the end the Catalans start throwing cushions from the stand. Joey Jones was on the bench and these cushions are hitting him on the back of the head, so he turns round and starts throwing them back. Bob calmly turns round and says to him: 'Hey Joey, will you sit down; you'll start another civil war'.

Phil Neal

Fantastic times – I will miss him

He went through the card in football. He was the greatest of them all.

He played for Liverpool, he trained players, he treated them, he coached them and he managed them.

I just wish I had a better command of the English language to express exactly what I feel for the man.

He was always very modest but one thing is for sure, underneath he was very intelligent and had a great knowledge of football.

He could tell if someone was injured just by seeing them walk across a room.

Inside you could tell he was also very proud of the team's achievements.

His understanding of the game was simple and he got that across to the players and used to laugh at all those coaches who thought it was a very technical game.

Bob was one of the greatest and most successful managers in the history of British football.

We had some fantastic times together at Liverpool and I'll miss him.

Kenny Dalglish

Bob made me into a better player

No man had a bigger influence on my career than Bob Paisley. His knowledge of the game was fantastic and we could always talk to one another.

I don't know how he thought up that new role for me, but he realised for sure I'd lost my appetite up front. Despite my size, I was never a battering ram centre-forward.

Bob made me into a better player and he went on doing that for other lads at Liverpool.

Ray Kennedy

Good habits are taught by those who know the game

Liverpool are a great club to play for, with an exceptional managerial staff.

All they want you to do is play football and keep yourself fit.

Good habits are taught by people who really know the game and when you played you felt that you owed the club and the fans a duty to perform as good professionals – how often do you hear of a Liverpool player being sent off.

You don't realise what pressures are kept from you as a player until you become a manager yourself. Bob will enjoy retirement because he knows how to relax – and nobody deserves it more!

For what Bob Paisley has done, whoever follows him should be eternally grateful for his having left them such a great side.

Emlyn Hughes

Bob will say an emotional farewell

Bob Paisley has an outstanding knowledge of the game and his judgement of a player's nature and background to ensure harmony on and off the field is impeccable.

I consider myself very fortunate to have joined Liverpool.

The tactical awareness of the man is to be admired. Who can forget the brilliant, vital decision to bring in Howard Gayle against Bayern Munich, who ran their defence ragged and then was pulled off?

In my five years at Anfield, Bob Paisley has shown emotion only when we have won something.

There will be plenty of emotion when he retires.

Graeme Souness

Former brickie who just got on with the job

My earliest recollection of him was when a gateman was complaining to the groundsman about a girder sticking out at one of the turnstiles. Bob, a former brickie, was standing nearby. He turned to me and said: 'You're a strong lad, come with me' and we sawed off the offending piece of the girder. His biggest asset was refraining from joining the loud-mouthed brigade when he is winning – he just got on with the job. I always laugh when I think about Bob because he was a funny man. I think I'll remember Bob most for his team meetings. They were legendary.

Tommy Smith

Paisley motivation got me on road to recovery

I was 20 years old, had returned home that day from having a cartilage operation and was feeling rather sorry for myself that evening when the telephone rang. It was Bob Paisley asking whether I'd been out driving my car yet. I told him that my knee was too sore and he told me that the day he returned home after a similar operation, he had removed an old, heavy grate and replaced it with a new one. Later that same evening, I was driving around Kirkby in my car and the next day I reported to Anfield. It only dawned on me afterwards that my pride had been triggered!

Phil Thompson

The best advice I've ever been given

The time I best remember Bob was when I went in to ask why I wasn't playing in the first team. I'd played seven or eight games without scoring, but I felt I'd been doing well.

I plucked up the courage to see him and he told me I was out of the side because I wasn't getting enough goals.

He said he'd seen me in training and that I was passing the ball too often.

I told him I was doing that because Liverpool were a passing team. But he said that sometimes I had to be greedy and go for goal. If I didn't, I wouldn't have a future at Liverpool. Bob kept stressing the importance of scoring. I'd been playing to get away from the club, and I thought Bob would put me on the transfer list, but he didn't. After that talk I became more selfish.

I scored something like six goals in two or three reserve games, and when David Johnson got injured Bob gave me my chance in the first team again. That example shows how he knew how to handle people. Telling me to be more selfish was the best advice I've been given.

Ian Rush

He got excellent value from his buys

I never doubted his coaching ability – he knew his goalkeeping too. After talks with Bob Paisley, 'Shanks' would get the message over and anything that he missed, Bob would put in.

He has a superb assessment of players, resulting in no bad buys and getting excellent value from those under his guidance without the need to fill their head with tactical ideas.

Ray Clemence

No job too small

He served Liverpool nobly for 43 years in various capacities – and that is essentially the greatness of the man. No job was too small for such a marvellous servant.

Bob Paisley stands for dignity, humility and all that is best in British sport. I am proud to think of him as a friend.

**Denis Compton,
cricketer**

Same modest man

I first met Bob some 20 years ago when I helped to promote boxing at the Liverpool Stadium. Bob was a keen boxing fan in those days. Since then he has won one football honour after another, yet he's still the same modest man.

**Great friend,
Ray Peers**

Bob was his own man

Bob either saw I had something to offer on the coaching side – or that I couldn't play! He encouraged me to go into coaching. Bob, Joe Fagan and Ronnie Moran were always helping me.

They saw me as a 25-year-old lad coaching a team and I could always go to them if I had a problem. On occasions I would tell Bob I wasn't sure of something and he'd tell me I wasn't the only one. I learned that anyone who thinks they know everything about football is kidding you. What Bob said was quite fragmented sometimes, but he always got his point across. What he told people was so simple it could be said in one or two words. His results showed that he could make a point or two!

It doesn't surprise me what Bob achieved because he worked with Shanks and had Joe and Ronnie to lean on. For me, the first manager was Shanks. I thought that the next one had to be like him, but it doesn't have to be that way. Bob could never be another 'Shanks.' Nor did he want to be. But he went about his job well, as the number of trophies shows.

Roy Evans

Team spirit is down to his style

When he took over as manager, he didn't really want to, but the club offered him the job and he just got on with it. His judgement of players in buying and how long to keep them at the club; the way in which new players are welcomed; the great spirit that prevails in the dressing room and on the field are all testimony to his individual style.

Ronnie Moran

He took Cup snub like a real man

My first memory of him was when he was not chosen for the 1950 Cup Final and my Dad and Uncle Tom enthused about how he took the decision like a real man – praise indeed from two tough dockers.

Tom O'Connor, comedian

No gold bracelets for rock-hard Bob

Not for him the loud mouth and gold bracelets. He gets on with the job in hand and lets the team do the talking on the pitch. I once played against him in a charity match at Anfield for Gerry Byrne's testimonial and during the course of the game I ran straight into him. I can tell you it was like running into a brick wash-house. He was bloody hard. And I tell you something: He'll be bloody hard to follow.

Jimmy Tarbuck, comedian

Great men harness power of youth

I first met Bob Paisley when he treated my bruised hands with modern treatment and his knowledge of physiotherapy. I just sat there in the treatment room just thrilled to be at Anfield.

As a Liverpool lad, I have been inspired by the support of Liverpool people, a spirit which lifts a man to greater things. The fans have helped Liverpool FC over the years with a dynamic man at the top – a winning combination.

One of my favourite memories is the day, soon after my world title defence against Len Hutchins, when I rode into town on the open-top bus with the Liverpool team as they returned from Rome with the European Cup.

It takes great men of wisdom to harness the power and skills of youth and greatness is a quality endowed on Bob Paisley. He is the sort of man you need in your corner.

John Conteh, boxer

Thanks for your great teams, Bob

Since 1931, football has been my hobby and I go to every match home and away – including Europe and the World Club Championship in Japan – and the wife says that I think more of Liverpool than I do of her!

Nothing pleases me more than to be in the supporters' club at another ground and listen to them praising my team.

It's through the efforts of Bob Paisley that we receive these accolades and the opposing team gets the best gate of the season.

Thanks Bob for giving me the pleasure of following the best team that this country has ever produced.

Bill Donnelly, Life-long fan

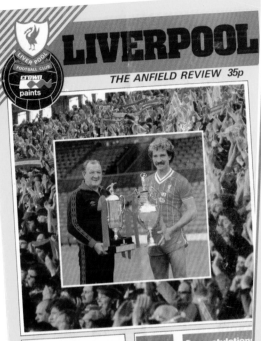

LIVERPOOL

THE ANFIELD REVIEW 35p

LEAGUE DIVISION 1
LIVERPOOL v. ASTON VILLA
Saturday, 7th May, 1983
Kick-off 3 p.m.

TODAY'S MATCH SPONSORS

Congratulations Bob
British TELECOM Liverpool

See page 15

THE FINAL TEAM TALK

by *Bob Paisley*

I EXPECT I shall have mixed emotions as the final whistle blows this afternoon, for it will signal not only the end of our last League game here this season, but my last appearance at Anfield in charge of team affairs. I've tried to imagine just how I shall feel, as I walk into the dressing-room after the match ... but I'll know for certain when that moment comes.

In the meantime, I have no doubts about one thing: so many people have made this job easier for me to do, at various times during the past nine years, that I wonder now why I ever hesitated in taking it on. In fact, I have come to realise that the easiest thing about the job was the way that people went out of their way to be of genuine assistance.

As for the hardest thing during my time as manager ... that's an easy one to answer. Quite simply, it was reaching a decision to pack the job in! But, having made that decision, I also accepted that everything—good and bad—has to come to an end sooner or later.

You cannot please all of the people all of the time, and I know that I haven't always suited everyone in this city, or even at this club; but, having conceded this, let me just add that fortunately, the people who from time to time have been critical of my actions turned out to be very much in a minority. And I'd like to think that I've never reached the stage where the critics and I were never going to be on speaking terms again!

I was asked this week what being a freeman of the city of Liverpool involved, and I answered—jokingly—that it meant, in my case, being given a free transfer! Seriously, I am very sensible of all the honours which have come my way while I have lived and worked in Liverpool, and I am not merely paying lip service to this club when I say that I regard most of the honours as being for Liverpool F.C. as well as for myself.

Now and again, there are odd things which annoy or frustrate you—I'm only human, like everyone else—but I can honestly say that never once have I regretted taking the managerial job, diffident though I might have been when I was asked to follow Bill Shankly.

I said at the outset that I hoped the team would do the talking for me, and I think I can fairly claim that, right the way through, the players who have worn Liverpool's colours during my spell as manager have done just that. Equally, I would be the first to pay tribute to the backing I have had not only from the players, but from everyone on the staff.

There have been times when I have felt, sincerely, that the players and the staff were making the job look ridiculously easy for me ... and I must say, also, that the Liverpool supporters have been of tremendous help. I've had so many messages of goodwill from our fans that it would be impossible to reply personally to them all ... so, please, take this as a heartfelt thank-you from me ... to everyone.

WE print without further need for comment a letter from a Watford fan, Mrs. Cathy Purrington. "I look forward to our match against Liverpool on May 14—I know it will be a marvellous game—and I am sure the Watford supporters will give Mr. Paisley as good a send-off as the Liverpool supporters. He is greatly admired, and I wish him all the best when he retires as manager."

Behind his desk for the last time: Pages from Bob Paisley's final team talk and a tribute in the match programme from Liverpool's last home game of the 1982/83 season against Aston Villa, which ended in a 1-1 draw

THE FINAL

"My ultimate ambition is to take over from Bob Paisley and Liverpool as undisputed masters of the English game and, subsequently, Europe. In terms of his record, Bob is the greatest manager of all time. He took over a superb club and team, but he has taken them forward to even greater achievements. I realise I'm setting myself a hell of a target in wanting to take over, but that is the only way I can think ..."
Manchester United manager RON ATKINSON, on the eve of the Milk Cup final.

SALUTE...

"I watched Liverpool beating Manchester United at Wembley, and even from those televised highlights it was clear to see what a great and complete team they are ... The record of their manager, Bob Paisley, is second to none; he has swept up the honours at home and abroad with a string of achievements that will be almost impossible to beat."
Manchester City manager JOHN BENSON, on the day Liverpool won 4-0 at Maine Road.

"Football's most successful manager has earned official recognition as a Master of Science. Liverpool University are to confer an honorary degree on Bob Paisley, the man who has led Liverpool F.C. through a period of success unprecedented in the English game. Paisley said, 'I think it's for Liverpool Football Club as much as for me.'"
Sports-news item in January of this year.

CHRISTINE WAS BOB PAISLEY'S ONLY DAUGHTER. HER FATHER WAS WORSHIPPED BY THOUSANDS FOR THE JOB THAT HE DID BUT BOB WOULD BE A HERO TO HER FOR DIFFERENT REASONS

Growing up with A LEGEND

> Bob Paisley was freed from the pressures of managing the country's top football club when he resigned after nine seasons in charge in 1983. He handed over the reins to Joe Fagan but still remained involved as a director of the club. It would be a very different kind of existence after the demands of life in the Liverpool hotseat

Hang about Charlie! What's this about the 'POMO' position?

From newspaper cutting, September/October 1983

(The article refers to the methods of FA Assistant Director of Coaching Charlie Hughes. Many of England's top managers attended a coaching course where the terms 'POMO' (Position Of Maximum Opportunity) and 'second six-yard box' were first utilised to the bemusement of many in attendance).

In case you are wondering why there are no names to go with these quotes, it's because of a little clause called 'bringing the game into disrepute', the article started.

All of the managers I spoke with who attended the course were happy to talk about the experience.

'Best laugh I've had for years'...'had us all in stitches'...'you should have heard what my players said when I told them about the POMO'.

It got great reviews, but without exception the managers added: 'For God's sake, don't quote me by name. You can't take the mick out of the FA Assistant Director of Coaching and not get done, can you?'

One man who didn't mind being quoted, however, was Bob Paisley.

"Aye, lad, these merchants have been at it for years. Wrap things up in fancy phrases and try to baffle you with science," he

CHRISTINE'S STORY

Bob's daughter Christine no longer carries the Paisley name, giving no clue to people that don't know her of the special memories she holds dear of growing up with the country's most successful football manager.

She now works as a nursery teacher in Derby, having first moved to the Midlands to take up a college course. During his retirement, Bob often made trips to see his daughter, enjoying the opportunity to spend time in a city where he could walk in relative anonymity.

Christine still keeps her collection of miniature dolls brought home by Bob after Liverpool had played a game on the continent. She recently spoke on local radio of her pride after the campaign to get her father knighted for his footballing achievements gathered pace in 2007.

Christine with daughter Kirsty and Jessie at a family wedding in 2005

Football first, weddings second – but we never questioned it

Father of the bride: A proud day with Christine in October, 1982

I managed to get married twice when Dad was the manager. We had to plan the wedding when Liverpool weren't likely to be playing.

It was either moved to the Monday or the Friday, when my brothers got married.

After the wedding, it was straight back to Liverpool the next day. I remember that I went to a League Cup match at Anfield for the honeymoon and we got passes into the Ladies lounge.

We just accepted that we had to fit family occasions around Dad's job.

It was the way we were brought up. We never questioned it.

said. "Couldn't stand it myself. Kept on about getting men into the third half of the field. When I went to school we only had two halves.

"First time I remember it creeping into the game was when Bill Shankly was still manager and we played against a London team at Anfield and were giving them a right hiding.

"Suddenly their coach screamed from the bench 'Apply the principles.' And Shanks turned to me and said: 'Bloody hell, Bob, we're in trouble now. They're going to apply the principles'.

"We had a good chuckle but I'm afraid those blokes are taking over the game.

"Football is simple and the best way to talk about it is in simple language. If players can't understand what you are talking about, they'll just ignore you."

'Did you use windscreen men at Liverpool?' I asked Paisley casually.

"What, you mean those fellas in garages who clean your car down?" he asked.

'No, Bob, they are players who patrol just in front of the central defenders, acting as a sort of windscreen, see?'

"What a load of cobblers. Who told you all this stuff?"

'It comes from a man named Charlie Hughes.'

"Charlie who?"

Bob's blast from the past!

Daily Express, January 31, 1984

Bob Paisley OBE faced a real 'This Is Your Life' situation at the weekend – a meeting with a man he thought was dead – and whose life he saved!

The surprise guest at a football writers' dinner honouring English soccer's most successful manager was his ex-war-time battery commander, Capt. John Carslake, a Solihull solicitor.

They last met in Italy 40 years ago during a mortar bomb attack,

Sherwood Forest and a bad case of mistaken identity!

when there was a direct hit on the slit trench where they were sheltering.

Gunner Paisley, now a Liverpool director, escaped unhurt and carried his badly wounded officer to a casualty station. Reliving that day, he said: "I have always believed he had been killed in that action. I can still hardly credit that he came through it!

"I can still remember every detail of the day, including the fact that I was wearing gym shoes in case I had to make a run for it!

"And that Capt. Carslake, in charge of a new unit I'd just joined, sent me back for a steel helmet before I drove him in a jeep for a front-line inspection of anti-tank guns. After that shell landed, I genuinely thought he had had it!"

Top English soccer expert in town

Jakarta Post, February 6, 1984

Top English soccer expert in town

BOB PAISLEY

JAKARTA (JP): "There should be another system in coaching Asian footballers in view of their averagely shorter posture than their counterparts in Europe and America," said Bob Paisley.

That was the initial comment of the noted English soccer expert when asked by the press here Tuesday about what method will be

"There should be another system in coaching Asian footballers in view of their averagely shorter posture than their counterparts in Europe and America," said Bob Paisley.

I've just been to Sherwood Forest with a school party and it reminded me of a story about Dad.

He used to come and visit me in Derby and we used to go there when my son was a baby.

One day he came when he was retired and he was pushing the pram along when this man stopped him and said: 'I know you!'

Dad was quite used to getting stopped because of who he was, but the man wasn't quite sure, although he recognised his face.

Then he said: "I do know you – you're that butcher from Mansfield!"

Dad just said 'yes' and carried on walking.

He used to like coming to Derby because he felt he could be more anonymous. He could push his grandchildren along and wasn't getting stopped all the time.

Completing the family: With Dad, Graham and Robert in 1954

That was the initial comment of the notable English soccer expert when asked by the press here about what method will be most appropriate to train Asian soccer players.

"My main purpose by coming down here is to give soccer clinics to the Indonesian football coaches," he told the Post upon arrival at Halim Perdanakusama airport.

"I've never known Indonesian footballers. This is my first visit here and I haven't the chance yet to learn about them," he added.

Paisley, himself a leading footballer in his heyday, is making the visit under joint sponsorship of the ALL Indonesian Football Federation and a cigarette company BAT.

He will watch Indonesian players in action as part of efforts here to improve standards of play.

In Jakarta, Paisley will provide a coaching class on Thursday, then he will go to Bandung to give a coaching session on Friday.

After other coaching sessions, he will wind up his Indonesian tour with another soccer lecture and clinic (see photos below).

'DAD WAS QUITE USED TO GETTING STOPPED BECAUSE OF WHO HE WAS, BUT THE MAN WASN'T QUITE SURE, ALTHOUGH HE RECOGNISED HIS FACE. THEN HE SAID: 'I DO KNOW YOU — YOU'RE THAT BUTCHER FROM MANSFIELD!''

› **Busy Bob Paisley**

Indonesia Times, February, 1984

English football expert Bob Paisley conducted a coaching clinic at the Senayan Stadium which was attended by a number of Indonesian coaches and soccer players (see below).

Diplomat Paisley preaches Reds' gospel in Holy Land

**Football Echo
By Mark Gaier
May 12, 1984**

(A review of Liverpool's preparations for the 1984 European Cup final – in Israel)

Bob Paisley's visit...received the sort of media coverage normally reserved for Heads of State and Hollywood superstars. "Welcome Bob" was the half page greeting (in English) from the Hebrew popular tabloid Hadashot which had organised the visit.

From the moment Paisley stepped foot on Israeli soil he became the centre of attention as airport workers and travellers alike converged to shake his hand. "Avi, you look well and you've lost weight!" exclaimed Bob as he embraced his former player, Avi Cohen who was part of the welcoming party, before he disappeared into a mass of eager reporters.

The next morning, watching a training session by league leaders Beitar Jerusalem, Paisley confessed an interest in their ›

Signing autographs (top) at Christine's wedding and a guest at St Hilda's

Star turn at school and picking out a tune on the organ

young centre-forward, Eli Ohana.
He also had kind words for the idol of the Jerusalem public Uri Malmilian and the overall technique of the Beitar players.

Emerging from a discussion with Beitar coach, David Shweitzer, it was now the turn of Paisley the diplomat to shine as he paid a courtesy call on President Chaim Herzog. A big follower of football, Herzog was told by Paisley that Avi Cohen could have been a regular in the Anfield side, possessing all the necessary attributes, save for too little patience which Paisley described as "a pity" (see scrapbook page below).

Irish eyes on Paisley

**From cutting,
October 27, 1984**

Officials of the Irish FA are contemplating another approach to former Liverpool manager Bob Paisley in the hope that he will agree to take over as supremo of the Eire national team.

The Irish FA made a previous approach to Mr Paisley two years ago, when he had just announced his impending retirement as manager, but on that occasion he declined.

He was still waiting to see how he would feel when his management duties ended and turned down other offers of employment from outside sources.

Musical: With grandchildren Kirsty and Stuart on the organ at home

I played the flute at school. He would come along to speech days at the Philharmonic and things like that if he didn't have a match.

I've got a friend who says that her Dad went with him to the pub after a speech night but I don't think Mum would have allowed that! If I was in a play, he would be there. He was very supportive.

I went to St Hilda's school and he would come along and open the summer fete when he could and bring an autographed ball.

He liked to play a bit on the organ himself. He was very good at picking out a tune, he had a bit of an ear for certain tunes.

He did quite well for someone who had no musical background.

Making the most

**The People
May 20, 1985**

Bob Paisley was the only manager to pick up an award – and he couldn't have been more shocked or delighted.

Paisley, the ex-Liverpool boss, was the first man to receive a special Eric Morecambe Memorial Award for services to football.

"I thought I was only here to help carry Kenny Dalglish's trophies so I couldn't believe my ears when the award to me was announced," said Paisley.

"And the fact that it is in memory of Eric makes it even more of an honour for me.

"My first match as Liverpool manager was at Luton and five minutes before the kick-off our dressing room door burst open and there was Eric shouting 'You're a load of rubbish.'

"We all fell about laughing and we became firm friends over the years."

Bob's boost for Kenny

**Liverpool Echo
May 31, 1985**

(Kenny Dalglish's appointment as the club's first-ever player manager came in the wake of the Brussels disaster. At 34 he would be the youngest boss in Division One, although that was balanced by the fact that Bob Paisley would

Holding the baby: With grandchild Helen in 1979

He used to train on Christmas Day in the morning. We'd open our presents then he'd come back at lunchtime.

Quite often on Christmas night he'd have to go away again and stay at a hotel if Liverpool had a game on

Boxing Day, so we didn't always see that much of him.

But he made the most of it when he was there. He used to carry the turkey in at Christmas.

He always got it as a present from the club – all the staff got one but the

# of a festive feast

All together: With the family, Christmas 1979. Liverpool beat Manchester United 2-0 at Anfield the next day on the way to the title. Christine is standing on the far right

act as his consultant and right-hand man)

Paisley said: "I don't think it will succeed – I know it will. Kenny is a very special kind of person, who is football through and through.

"I look on this as a partnership, rather in the way that Bill Shankly and I were able to work together, and he was another great Scot of course. We used to talk things over, and sometimes we disagreed, but there was never any animosity about it.

"I believe it will be the same with Kenny, and if I can help him it should work out very well. In my view Kenny has something that is unique in football, and it would be a criminal waste if we hadn't made use of it.

"I know a lot of great players have not made it as managers, but few of them were as completely dedicated to the game as Kenny. He eats, drinks and sleeps football, without anyone telling him what to do, and has this uncanny knack of being able to involve other people.

"That isn't just on the field. He is valuable to us, on the training ground and in the dressing room. The only thing is, while he is still playing he needs someone to keep an eye on things from the outside and give him a second opinion."

The loneliest job in the world

FA Cup preview 1986
Daily Mirror,
May, 1986

Kenny Dalglish will sit down in his Anfield office this week and, with the stroke of a pen, break somebody's heart.

For the first time in a soccer life that has brough vast success, glamour and fame, the Liverpool boss will select a Cup final team and have to tell long-standing friends and team-mates: "Sorry, you'll miss Everton and Wembley."

Bob Paisley, the Godfather,

size of the turkey depended on how long you had been there so if you were polishing the boots or something like that, you might get one the size of a pigeon.

Obviously Dad got rather a large turkey after all the time he'd been at

Liverpool.

I have to say I was quite spoilt at Christmas. I got what I asked for, although it isn't like it is now.

We never thought of him not being there much at Christmas, we just accepted it because of his job.

knows the anguish and agony facing Dalglish. "He'll shed tears," says Bob. "Somebody has to get hurt, it's inevitable. It's the hardest task Kenny will ever face in his career. Choosing an FA Cup final team is the loneliest job in the world."

Paisley, the Anfield overlord, wants his successor to make history and become the first player manager to win at Wembley.

In the confines of his den, deep in the club's complex Paisley confided: "It's difficult but Kenny should write his own name first on the teamsheet. Liverpool with him playing are a much better side, it's as simple as that."

Such is the scramble for places that the final selection has become a manager's torment.

He'll know that Kevin MacDonald, Gary Gillespie, Mark Lawrenson, Steve McMahon, Paul Walsh, Sammy Lee and others will be taking one-eyed sleep.

"But Kenny should be out there and chasing that record," adds Paisley. "I would have some concern about his legs lasting the distance and the team problems he'll be carrying. His playing role is highly demanding and the day will be testing. But I want him to make history.

"As for those left out, well some may be so disappointed that they ask for transfers. I know how miserable they'll feel about missing Wembley. I've suffered

This time the family picture is from Christmas, 1982 – Bob's last as Liverpool manager. The Reds beat Manchester City 5-2 at Anfield on Boxing Day – and another title would be won

> that blow myself."

It has already been suggested that Paisley leads out Liverpool alongside Everton manager Howard Kendall – assuming that Dalglish plays.

His dignity emerged again when he remarked: "I'm not fussy. If Kenny is wearing his boots and I'm helping in some way then I'll go out in front. But that is the least of my thoughts."

He has been measured for a new club suit which could be taken as a clue.

Bob's job! Until Irish say 3 votes beat 9

The People, February 9, 1986

On Friday Republic of Ireland chairman Des Casey rang Liverpool to ask if they would release Bob Paisley for the part-time post. They agreed.

Paisley's name was added to the original short-list of Johnny Giles, Liam Tuohy and Jack Charlton and the secret vote was taken by the 18-man committee.

The result: Paisley 9, Giles 3, Tuohy 3, Charlton 3.

That left Paisley a clear winner. Well, he would have been anywhere else except in Ireland.

Because they decided to have another vote, eliminating Giles and Tuohy this time.

Then, before the final vote, one of the members made a plea that it would be wrong to give the job to someone who wasn't on the original short-list – Paisley.

That plea persuaded one of Paisley's supporters to change his mind.

The result of the vote?

Charlton 10, Paisley 8.

So the man who won the vote – the most successful manager of all-time – lost the job!

The final irony is that chairman Casey range former team manager Eoin Hand yesterday to ask if he would supply the new team manager with the players' telephone numbers!

> ### Unlucky break won't rule Bob out

**Liverpool Echo,
October 30, 1986**

Bob Paisley took a light session with a group of Liverpool's injured kids at Melwood yesterday ... and finished up with a broken ankle, writes Ken Rogers.

The most successful manager the game has ever known, an Anfield director these days as well as being the man Kenny Dalglish can lean on for advice in any situation was recovering at home today and reflecting on the irony of the situation.

Bob told me: "I was just putting the lads through some exercises and didn't even realise the extent of the problem. I was walking and then sat down to lunch. The phone went and when I tried to get up I realised that I couldn't put my foot down. It turned out that I had broken one of the bones in my ankle.

College lift with a bacon butty and getting a big Anfield surprise

Surprise: Bob Paisley is announced as new Liverpool manager in 1974

When I went away to college, it was an eye-opener to find that people supported other teams!

I was at college when Dad became manager and if I finished term on a Saturday, it didn't matter if there was a match, he would always pick me up. We would stop off at a transport café on the way back and he'd buy me a bacon butty. He'd always pick me up, he'd just fit it around the game and make sure he was back in time if Liverpool were playing.

We didn't know he was going to be manager. I was at a friend's wedding and when I came back my mum said to me: "Bill Shankly's resigned." And I said: "Is Dad going to be manager?" Mum just said: "Don't be so daft!"

So I told all my friends that he wasn't going to be manager.

I think we were the only people who were really surprised when it was announced that he was taking over.

I've never let my mum forget that!

"It made me think of the very first injury I had as a Liverpool player. I had signed from Bishop Auckland and we faced 13 games in a fortnight. We couldn't manage it so we had to concede two and play eleven.

"I broke that same ankle, although I had all summer to get it better. Over the years I always had to look after it because it niggled away at times."

He joked: "I won't be available for Saturday but the injury won't keep me away from Anfield. I will attend the next board meeting on crutches."

Big three have spoiled Mersey quality

Daily Mirror, November 5, 1986

"I've just one thing to say to the likes of Phil Neal, Chris Lawler and Geoff Twentyman – stop belly aching and biting the hand which fed you for so long," said Paisley in response to perceived negative comments in the press.

"You should be proud to have served such a great club – and don't forget you got well paid for it. The people I feel sorry for are the thousands of decent, ordinary folk on Merseyside.

"For many of them, whether they be Liverpudlians or Evertonians, football is their only escape from the poverty and deprivation in an area of massive unemployment. They are proud of Merseyside, and its clubs, so when well-to-do former players and employees start slinging mud it hurts them as well.

"Neal, Lawler and Twentyman all knew that there is nothing guaranteed in football. They were old enough to know that football is more uncertain than most jobs.

"If Liverpool was such a bad club why did they all stay for so long? If they didn't like it they could have packed it in at any time they wanted – or were the wages too good to resist?"

"I can still remember my humble beginnings and the

poverty in the pit villages of County Durham.

"I feel proud and privileged to have been able to be of service to a great club in a great city.

"It's a pity that other people have such short memories and have forgotten that they owe their own successes to Liverpool FC and Merseyside."

Wales may look to Paisley

From newspaper report by Peter Went

Mike England, sacked after eight years as manager of Wales, last night pointed the Principality towards a potential successor – while rumours circulated that former Liverpool manager Bob Paisley could take the job.

Paisley, Brian Clough and even Kenny Dalglish were among a book of names thrown up by the Welsh FA council.

Paisley lost out to Jack Charlton for the Republic of Ireland vacancy. He could emerge as a leading contender, with David Williams (Norwich player-coach) possibly, a track-suited assistant.

But the favourite remains Swansea boss Terry Yorath.

Paisley critical

From cutting, By Phil McNulty, January 22, 1988

(Liverpool were 15 points clear at the top of the table at the time)

Bob Paisley has fired a broadside at declining First Division standards.

Speaking at a young player of the month ceremony in Manchester, he said: "The present Liverpool team have probably got one of the biggest leads anyone has ever had.

"But I have got to say they have been aided and abetted by the poorest First Division I have seen in my years in the game.

Happy memories: On holiday in 1963 (above) and at Bournemouth in 1967 – business called for Dad

Seeing the stars and we're not all going on a summer holiday

a very warm welcome

Hope you will have a pleasant stay

With the Personal Compliments of

Willy

WILLY B. G. BAUER

Managing Director and General Manager

The Savoy
London

Telephone: 01-836 4343

The last family holiday we were all together was on a boat on the Thames during the week that is now the Spring Bank Holiday. Dad also went on club holidays in those days, which were holidays and not work.

There were other perks to Dad's job, though. We often got tickets for shows because Dad once helped this man who used to run the Empire and then the Palladium when he was a physio. The man used to say 'if it wasn't for your Dad, I would never have walked again!'

We also used to sometimes meet the stars afterwards, in their dressing rooms. I remember at the time I was fond of Cliff Richard and Mum said 'there's no point in going all the way down to London to see him unless we can meet him', so we did.

> 'I REMEMBER AT THE TIME I WAS FOND OF CLIFF RICHARD AND MUM SAID 'THERE'S NO POINT IN GOING ALL THE WAY DOWN TO LONDON TO SEE HIM UNLESS WE CAN MEET HIM', SO WE DID'

"Maybe the lack of European competition has taken the edge off the domestic game."

Paisley believes only Mersey giants Liverpool and Everton, along with Spurs, Arsenal, Manchester United and Nottingham Forest, have got title pedigree in the top flight.

He added: "But from that group I personally gauge that Liverpool's biggest threat will still come from Everton."

Liverpool manager Kenny Dalglish has rightly ignored comparisons between his present all-conquering side and earlier Anfield teams.

And Paisley added that comparison were virtually impossible to make, commenting: "The current side will probably play about 48 games this season. It's difficult to make comparisons with the teams that had to play about 72 games."

Paisley 'is just one of our contenders'

**Liverpool Echo
February 29, 1988**

Former Liverpool boss Bob Paisley is NOT the first choice of the Welsh FA to take over the manager's vacancy but "he has been interviewed," says secretary Alun Evans.

"Mr Paisley is only one of several candidates we've interviewed," said Evans.

"A shortlist has been drawn up, but it's simply untrue to say that Mr Paisley heads it.

"As with all the other candidates, Mr Paisley is entitled to a degree of confidentiality and we will respect that right.

"I don't expect to be in a position to make any formal announcement this week and will be giving the Welsh FA full council a full report on the situation."

Paisley continues to be linked with a number of management jobs since deciding to call time on his glittering Liverpool career.

We lack talent to be world beaters

**Liverpool Echo,
October 30, 1988**

Bob was keen to have his say on all manner of football matters after his retirement from the Anfield hotseat.

In October 1988, he took a dim view of England's World Cup hopes as they started their campaign for Italia 90.

He told the Liverpool Echo: "There isn't a great deal of talent around and what there is tends to be concentrated at a few big clubs.

"In the old days, you could ask someone to name his England team and there would only be a question mark over one or two places.

"Now there are a good many players of much the same standard and very few who you could call genuine stars. It is a thankless job being the England manager.

"There is no shortage of people only too happy to tell him how to do his job but in the end he is out on his own and judged by the performance of players who he might not have intended to use in the first place.

"I think it would help if our clubs played less football, because I suspect many of our players are jaded when it comes to major international tournaments."

Bob joins the greats

**Liverpool Echo,
March 10, 1989**

Former Liverpool FC boss Bob Paisley joins the great men of the past 30 years next month at a Savoy Hotel dinner to raise money for Britain's three million disabled children and adults.

Mr Paisley, Man of the Year for 1983, will join other winners of the title including actor Sir John Mills, Enniskillen bomb hero Gordon Wilson, tycoon Richard

Messing about on the river: Christine recalls this Thames boating holiday in 1966 as the last the whole family spent together

> Branson and Zeebrugge ferry disaster hero Andrew Parker in a bid to raise £30,000.

Bob joins the greats

FORMER Liverpool FC boss Bob Paisley joins the great men of the past 30 years next month at a Savoy Hotel dinner to raise money for Britain's three million disabled children and adults.

Mr Paisley, Man of the Year in 1983, will join other winners of the title, including actor Sir John Mills, Enniskillen bomb hero Gordon Wilson, tycoon Richard Branson and Zeebrugge ferry disaster hero Andrew Parker in a bid to raise £30,000.

Our school interview with Bob Paisley

**Hetton Lyons Primary School newspaper
By Graham Field and
Paul Comby,
July 1989**

We wrote to Bob Paisley who was born in Hetton and who was manager of Liverpool and who is now a director of Liverpool. Here are his answers to our questions.

Q. Do you think there should be more leagues for young people at present?
A. I regret I am unable to answer this, as I don't know how many leagues are in existence.

Q. Do you think the present Liverpool team is as good as past Liverpool teams?
A. Yes, in its own way, as each team has different characteristics, depending on the personality of each player.

Q. Which has been the best Liverpool team?
A. It is difficult to make comparisons as situations vary over the years, for example in the teams I controlled as a manager, >

we played in Europe, thereby often having about 15 games extra, as well as having often six international players. Emlyn Hughes, for one, played 75 competitive games in one season.

Q. What does being a director involve?
A. It involves discussing and making decisions, the maintenance and welfare of the club in co-operation with the manager, who alone picks the team.

Q. Which teams did you play for locally?
A. Eppleton School, Hetton Juniors, Bishop Auckland.

Q. Were there any other well-known people playing then?
A. I remember Harry Potts who became manager of Burnley and lived in Hetton.

Q. Did you play for your school team?
A. Yes, I won 13 medals in three years.

Q. Do you think football is more exciting than when you were playing?
A. Football is always an exciting game when you are playing, whether at schoolboy or professional level.

Paisley in line to be boss again

Liverpool Echo, August 21, 1989

Bob Paisley has been invited to become a football manager again – for the day.
    The legendary former Liverpoool boss, now a club director at his beloved Anfield, has been asked to take charge of the combined Liverpool/Juventus under-21 team to play the Skol Northern League in their game at Newcastle's St James's Park to commemorate the Magpies' centenary year.

Bob'll fix it: With a Jim'll Fix It winner at Liverpool airport in the 1980s

Up and away: On a 1981 trip (left) and at the airport on route to St Etienne

Gifts from Europe

He always used to bring a present back when he'd been away with Liverpool. I was very lucky like that. I remember once me and Mum met him at Speke Airport like we sometimes did when they got back from a game in Europe.

I remember him walking across the tarmac with this great big box from France. It was a model café with miniature glasses and everything. I remember everyone had to play café with me for quite a long time after that. Another time he brought me

Dolls in their national dress were brought home from Europe for Christine

> **Ex-boss
> Bob reveals
> Anfield flaw**

**Liverpool Echo,
September 6, 1989**

Liverpool are still the light of Bob Paisley's life – but he's spotted one glaring weakness.

They don't do enough scouting for new talent.

Speaking in a new book called The Football Managers, Paisley says: "When Kenny Dalglish took over, I used to go off on trips – when there was something big happening.

"But now we're not being called out and this might be a fault.

"It doesn't matter whether you say yes or no about a player, you can always give an opinion. They're settling in now and forgetting people.

"There are things that are being left. It's surprising really but they'll find out soon enough!"

**Anfield salutes
king of the bosses**

**Liverpool Echo,
October 23, 1990**

British football's most successful manager in Europe was honoured yesterday when he officially opened the new Bob Paisley Suite at Anfield.

Paisley was delighted at Liverpool's own personal tribute and said: "I didn't dream the club would do anything like this for me. When I look around I never realised we won so much.

"I certainly can't grumble at what we achieved here. I'm hoping to see Liverpool back in Europe next year because that is part of this club. Rome (in 1977) was the highlight for me."

made to measure

back a large doll from Italy that would walk when you pressed it. It was too big to put in our cabinet at home. He sometimes bought clothes too and he was very good at getting sizes right. He bought Mum a suit from Germany once. He would look

at a shop assistant that was about the same size and he would say 'I want one that size' and they would always fit. He never shopped for clothes at home because he got given so many things like suits and shoes. Mum did all the shopping for the basics.

Reds give Bob a room of his ...

Reds' top tribute to King Bob

Liverpool Echo, October 22, 1990

The Liverpool Echo took the opportunity to interview Paisley as the club announced its intention to honour their former boss with the 'Bob Paisley Suite' at Anfield.

Paisley spoke honestly about his time at Liverpool past and present . . .

Paisley on being reserve team manager:

"I told the boss (Bill Shankly) I was only interested in picking players who were interested in winning, whatever their reputation.

"He didn't take it very seriously but the players responded well and we won the Central League for the first time in the club's history.

"Suddenly everyone wanted to play in the reserves, because the first team were not winning anything at the time."

Paisley on his relationship with manager Kenny Dalglish:

"I tell him what I think and he's free to agree or disagree and do

Painting Paris red and kicking the Cup through a hotel door!

Allez Les Rouges! On the coach with husband Ian

I remember walking around Paris before the European Cup final in 1981 and seeing red and white everywhere we went. We travelled there in one of the club coaches which was not the directors' but probably the next one down.

It was quite a long journey because we travelled from Derby to Liverpool and then on to Paris, arriving at midnight. I remember we circled round and round for ages because we couldn't find our hotel.

We spent the day before going around Paris. We met Mum and her friend, who were on a whistle-stop tour. We asked them to take a photo of us but they said they were in too much of a rush, they had to get to the Champs Elysees next!

It was a great atmosphere at the

match and then afterwards we had our own party in the hotel. I don't think I spoke to Dad on the night as he was in a different hotel.

When they won in 1978, I was teaching in Liverpool and Dad took the Cup to the school. There didn't seem to be much security around in those days. I have a picture of him walking across the schoolyard holding the Cup.

I remember in 1974 when they won the FA Cup. For some reason, he had it and brought it back to the hotel. When he came into our room he had his hands full of lots of things and he ended up having to kick the Cup through the door! He wasn't one for keeping medals. Whenever he had three of one, he gave us one each. He kept his medals in a box in the loft.

> just what he likes. Kenny is his own man just as Bill (Shankly) was and there is no malice between us."

Paisley on Liverpool's success:

"This is a great club and not just because we have won so much. I can remember it in the hard times when we were in the Second Division and it was the same honest, family club then.

"Liverpool has not been spoiled by success, nor has it been undermined by disaster."

Anfield farewell

Liverpool Echo, February 7, 1992

Bob Paisley today ended his official association with Liverpool after more than half a century of devoted service.

The most successful manager in the Reds' history resigned from the Board through ill health but has been awarded a life vice-presidency by the club for his loyalty and outstanding achievements.

In a letter to the club, Paisley stated he could no longer maintain his place as an active member of the Liverpool board.

"I have served the club for over 50 years and to be elected to the board was the final accolade."

Reds chairman David Moores said: "He has served Liverpool Football Club in almost every capacity for more than 50 years and football has no equal in terms of management and prize winning.

"But Bob was more than a record silverware winner.

Reds on tour: In Paris in 1981. Also pictured with Christine's husband is brother Graham, wife Sandie and a friend

"His firm but gentle approach earned him the respect of everyone in football. His name will run synonomously with Liverpool.

"His knowledge of players and the game is unsurpassed but his modesty and dignity became overwhelming forces as he led this club from one triumph to another.

"Although Bob is not enjoying the best of health at the moment, we hope he can attend some home games and we are looking forward to seeing him. The board has made him a life vice-president."

Red manager Graeme Souness added: "I would say I learned more about football from Bob Paisley than any person I worked under.

"He's arguably the greatest servant this club has ever had."

Thanks, Bob! You did us proud

Liverpool matchday programme v Bristol Rovers, Tuesday, February 11th, 1992

The long and distinguished career of Bob Paisley came to an end when he resigned from the Liverpool Board of Directors earlier this month.

His letter to the club he served proudly for more than half a century read: 'Owing to ill health I can no longer maintain my place as an active board member of Liverpool FC.

Time to reflect: Bob is pictured on the pitch at the end of the match at the Parc Des Princes in which Liverpool defeated Real Madrid 1-0 to claim Paisley's third European Cup. It is one of the family snaps from the trip that now takes pride of place in son Graham's scrapbook

'I thank all my fellow board members for the pleasure it has been to work with them.'

His Anfield half century is unlikely to be equalled. He had served as a player, coach, trainer, physio, assistant manager, manager and, of course, director.

Simplicity, dignity and a deep knowledge of players and football were his main attributes. His quiet nature became an enormous strength.

Supporters, no doubt, will want to voice their special message to the man who carried on from Bill Shankly and built an empire: "Thanks for the memories, Bob."

Paisley makes Great Escape

Liverpool Echo, February 18, 1992

(This episode was recalled as part of an Echo series after Bob retired from the LFC board):

Bob Paisley had a lucky near miss with a Japanese PoW camp during the Second World War.

He had arrived at Anfield early in 1939 and played just two reserve games before the League competition was put into cold storage.

IT WAS A GREAT ATMOSPHERE AT THE MATCH AND THEN AFTERWARDS WE HAD OUR OWN PARTY IN THE HOTEL. I DON'T THINK I SPOKE TO DAD ON THE NIGHT AS HE WAS IN A DIFFERENT HOTEL'

Dad had so much it was sad that he

Paisley was called up to join the 73rd Regiment of the Royal Artillery at Tarporley.

He recalled: "The battery I was in went to the Far East. I should have gone with them but was transferred to another battery because I was the regimental soccer captain. That was a bit of luck because my unit was captured soon after it arrived and spent the rest of the war in a prisoner of war camp."

Paisley then served with Field Marshall Montgomery's Desert Rats, serving as a driver to a reconnaissance officer and fighting his way through North Africa, Sicily and Italy.

"We did manage a few games in Egypt but there was no chance to play any organised football before I came out," he recalled.

"It was a matter of starting all over again in 1946 after a six-year break."

Kop of the lot – Dalglish was Reds' greatest

Liverpool Echo, February 18, 1992

Paisley reminisced in an article with Ian Hargraves how he captured the signing of Kenny Dalglish from Celtic in 1977:

"We were lucky to have a very good relationship with the Celtic manager Jock Stein," he recalled. "We often chatted with Jock about football.

"We had been interested in Kenny for a long time, because we knew how good he could be, and Jock was good enough to tip us off when Kenny told him that he wanted to try his luck away from Glasgow.

"The news could not have come at a better time because Kevin Keegan had just left and we were looking for a replacement.

"I know people criticised us for paying so much money (he cost £440,000) but we had just sold Kevin for even more and had it available. Liverpool have always believed in investing their cash in

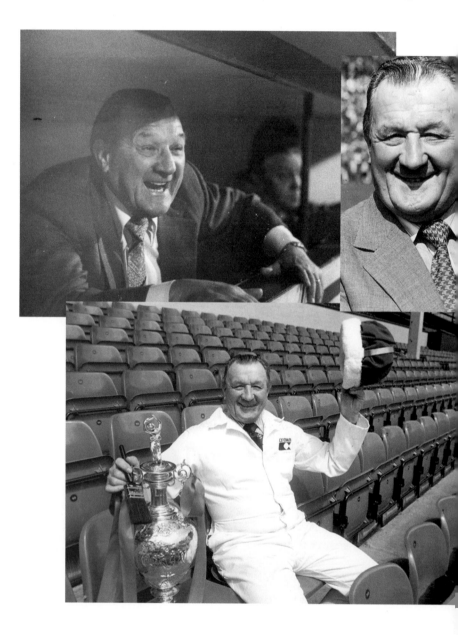

The worst thing about the illness for me was the fact that Dad lost his memory.

It was especially sad because someone like him had so many wonderful memories.

I feel sad for my children that they didn't get to know him better but the good thing is that they feel they know him through the many videos and books that have been done.

It's great that they can get to know him through them.

He loved playing with the grandchildren. He used to have a slide in the front room that he would play with them on.

He'd even go on it himself sometimes with the children and occasionally get stuck.

to look back on – lost his memories

'I FEEL SAD FOR MY CHILDREN THAT THEY DIDN'T GET TO KNOW HIM BETTER BUT THE GOOD THING IS THAT THEY FEEL THEY KNOW HIM THROUGH THE MANY VIDEOS AND BOOKS'

players and I don't think anyone could say that we did not get value for money.

"He had this rare quality of being able to know where the other players were without even looking and of being able to find them with a perfect pass. He was a tremendous individual player himself but what made him so exceptional was the fact that he could make others play too."

Talent spotter supreme

Liverpool Echo, February 19, 1992

One of Bob Paisley's greatest attributes as a manager was that he was a good player picker.

He made an amazing number of successful signings and although some of the newcomers were already stars, there were plenty of other players who were comparitively unknown until Liverpool got to work on them.

His first signing was one of the latter. He picked up Phil Neal from Northampton soon after taking over from Bill Shankly.

At much the same time, Paisley plucked young full back Roy Evans out of the reserves and told him to start concentrating on coaching instead.

Evans had been a schoolboy international and was still only 25 but Paisley pointed out that while he could never hope to hold down a regular place, he had a real future as a reserve team trainer.

With Evans in charge, Liverpool again charged up the Central League and picked up the championship in his first season in charge.

Paisley's three most spectacular signings were probably the three great Scots: Kenny Dalglish, Graeme Souness and Alan Hansen. Dalglish's signing was probably the greatest coup of all and has been justified a score of times since but the capture of Souness was almost equally important.

Playing alongside Souness in

> midfield was another vital signingTerry McDermott, a cheerful Scouser who went on to be named Footballer of the Year.

Alan Kennedy also made a big impression and former Evertonian David Johnson was another Paisley signing, this time from Ipswich.

With the break up of the 1979 title side, Paisley moved into the transfer market again. He bought Mark Lawrenson for £900,000, a great deal of money at the time, but that money was soon repaid as he proved himself able to play brilliantly in half a dozen positions.

Bruce Grobbelaar was acquired from Vancouver Whitecaps and Ian Rush was of course, one of Paisley's most successful signings. Bought from Chester for a mere £300,000 he was slow to live up to his promise until Paisley gave him a sharp reminder that he was expected to score goals, not just create them.

Towards the end of his career, Steve Nicol was snapped up from Ayr for £300,000 and Ronnie Whelan was acquired as one of several teenage Irishmen who have gone on to become international stars.

Paisley's success rate was phenomenally high and he always seemed able to spot potential early and to spot players who would fit into the traditional Liverpool pattern.

A man who believed passionately in balance, he created his great teams like a man completing a jigsaw puzzle, fitting in piece after piece with infinite care.

Head start at Palace

From LFC programme 1994-95 (March)

The conversation was sombre during the half-time interval of the Coca-Cola Cup semi-final game at Anfield.

Liverpool had made little impression on the Crystal Palace defence as they battled to secure

'Sir' Bob . . . and people still want to shake my hand

I got called into the local radio station to speak on the breakfast show about the campaign to get Dad knighted.

Lots of people were signing the petition, all of the school staff were putting their name on.

It's amazing to think that even though he's been dead 11 years, all those people are still thinking of him. It's heart-warming.

Whenever people find out who my Dad is, they say 'wasn't he a lovely man' and they want to shake my hand.

I tell them that it wasn't me who won all those things – I can't take the glory.

'IT'S AMAZING TO THINK THAT EVEN ALL THOSE PEOPLE ARE STILL

> a lead to take to Selhurst Park in the second leg.

At this point Ray.Peers, a committed Liverpool supporter, produced a flat cap and announced: "We'll be all right now, lads. We'll get a goal in the second half."

Even before he added the words "You know whose cap this is," recognition was dawning.

It had appeared on a score of photographs during the club's most glorious years, worn by a modest man with more to boast about than any other manager in football.

The cap was a gift from Bob Paisley, Ray's friend for 40 years, who wore it at grounds all over Britain and Europe.

These days Bob is prevented by illness from appearing at matches, but his sons Graham and Robert presented the cap to Ray during the game against QPR last month. Ray tried it for size. It fitted...and minutes later the Reds, who had been chasing an equaliser, scored through John Scales. A superstition was born then and gained weight against Palace, although Bob's cap left it late before Robbie Fowler got the crucial goal.

"Bob was the most modest man I ever met," recalls Ray. "A friend in a million. I treasure his cap and I'll wear it for every game."

As Bob faded out of the headlines after his departure from Anfield, so Liverpool struggled to maintain their place at the top of the English football ladder. It wasn't as if they hadn't been warned during his time in the Anfield boardroom . . .

THOUGH HE'S BEEN DEAD 11 YEARS
THINKING OF HIM. IT'S HEART-WARMING'

Liverpool chairman John Smith reading from a statement at a press conference called over Paisley's comments in 1989

SPEAKING
his mind

BOB WASN'T ONE FOR USING THE PRESS TO MAKE A POINT. ONE UNCHARACTERISTIC OUTBURST SHOCKED THE CLUB AND LED THE FAMILY TO BELIEVE THAT NOT ALL WAS WELL

**Daily Mirror
March, 1989**

Bob the Director

It was March, 1989, and the Liverpool machine was not running as smoothly as it should have been. Injuries and lack of form had left the Reds struggling in the league and critics lining up to write off the glory days. It was also the cue for Paisley to point out where he thought things were going wrong. His family now believe that this episode in his life marked the onset of the Alzheimer's Disease that would, within three years, force him to quit the Anfield board

Bob . . . on transfer funds:

Liverpool need money to fund more top players coming in – but they're not going to get much for the lads who should be swept out. With the cash from Europe gone and games at Anfield having been postponed for TV, we're losing money all the time.

There are players who are holding up the progress of the youngsters, kids who should be coming through the reserves – but they're just not cottoning on.

Liverpool are not good enough – there's no room for sentiment Kenny!

By Bob Paisley

Liverpool are not the team they were. They are not good enough just now and it's going to take a lot of money to put things right.

There's no room for sentiment. I was a big softie until it came to what was good for the club. Then I could be as hard as nails.

And (Liverpool player manager) Kenny can't afford to let his heart rule his head. It's OK being the nice guy but he's got to get rid of some players before they start to believe they have still got a future at Liverpool. It's only fair to a player, however pleasant a man he might be, to tell him when his time is up and his career is finished at your club.

At least he can try and get himself organised with another team and pick up a few quid. But if he's no longer any use at Liverpool he should be on his way.

> '**KENNY CAN'T AFFORD TO LET HIS HEART RULE HIS HEAD. IT'S OK BEING THE NICE GUY BUT HE'S GOT TO GET RID OF SOME PLAYERS BEFORE THEY START TO BELIEVE THAY HAVE GOT A FUTURE AT LIVERPOOL. IT'S ONLY FAIR TO A PLAYER'**

On captaincy:

They need a really strong captain again, a forceful personality who'd be a voice of authority on the park. Graeme Souness was the last great skipper. He was in the same category as Ron Yeats, Emlyn Hughes, Phil Thompson – all men of determination and a big influence.

Alan Hansen is a loner like Kenny, a player wrapped up in his own game and not a strong man like Souness. You need to be strong with a side like ours.

If Graeme had been skipper at Wembley for the Wimbledon final (FA Cup final, 1988 – which Liverpool lost 1-0), when Vinny Jones kicked Steve McMahon, it would have been a different story. Souness would have given McMahon a jolt to get on with it – and would have made sure Vinny knew he had him to deal with if there was any more of it.

On Jim Beglin and Alan Hansen:

It looks to me like Alan Hansen and Jim Beglin won't make it back into our first team. Alan has been struggling since he was hurt in Spain on the pre-season tour and Jim has never completely recovered from breaking his leg so badly.

Hansen's 33 and time is against him too. He was down to play a few days ago but he cried off because he wasn't up to it ... the kindest thing would be for both of them to be allowed to go.

On the fitness of modern players:

The lads these days are just not strong enough. They're not as robust as they should be. And they don't play anywhere near the number of games we did when we were in Europe. Emlyn Hughes told me in 1977 he played 72 games in the season. Now they're playing 40-odd and running into all sorts of injuries and long term ones at that. Gary Gillespie is a superb player but he's in and out with injury. It's the same with young Barry Venison.

In the stands as a director and talking to the press while a manager

An apology – and offer to quit

Liverpool Echo, March 2, 1989

Bob Paisley has made his peace with the team, apologising for remarks he made about them in a national newspaper.

Paisley, 70, who offered to quit as a director following the reports in which he criticised manager Kenny Dalglish and several of his senior players, made his "I'm sorry" gesture as he visited the players in the dressing room after the 2-0 Anfield victory against Charlton.

Liverpool's board held a special meeting to discuss the articles, but did not accept his resignation, choosing to let him off with a reprimand.

Last night Dalglish broke his silence over the controversy, saying: "I have tremendous respect for Bob Paisley. He was instrumental in bringing me here and was always a big help when I first became manager.

"Anyone connected with Liverpool Football Club must respect his achievements, but at the same time, I could not condone the articles that appeared in the newspaper."

Two winners: Paisley with new signing Dalglish in 1977

'ANYONE CONNECTED WITH LIVERPOOL FOOTBALL CLUB MUST RESPECT HIS ACHIEVEMENTS, BUT AT THE SAME TIME, I COULD NOT CONDONE THE ARTICLES THAT APPEARED'

Making up: John Aldridge and Bob Paisley in 1988

Making peace with Kop striker

It wasn't the first time that Paisley had landed himself in hot water because of his views while a Liverpool director.

Newspaper comments attributed to the former Liverpool manager criticised Anfield striker John Aldridge in 1988 and Aldridge hit back in a book.

But both men put the matter behind them and shook hands on the whole affair during a chat in the Anfield dressing room.

Aldridge, talking to the Liverpool Echo's Ken Rogers, said: "I love Liverpool. The last thing I wanted to do was cause any upset because the club is the only thing that matters, not my pride or Bob's. We had a good chat about it. I was simply defending myself because I was hurt and he understands that."

Paisley also stressed that he didn't want to in any way damage the club's reputation.

He said: "After being with Liverpool for 50 years as a player, manager and director, there can be no question where my loyalty lies and I would be heartbroken if I believed the club felt I was being vindictive.

"It is completely stupid because all I did was give my honest opinion about Aldridge's playing ability and the quality of the opposition Liverpool faced last season.

"I merely said that I wouldn't have bought Aldridge and expressed the view that although he is a good goalscorer, he had his limitations.

"As for me being jealous of Kenny Dalglish's record as manager, that is almost too daft for words.

"I'm very proud of Kenny because I brought him to the club as a player. We are not bosom pals and we have our difference of opinion but we had a good working relationship."

No more interviews but club won't accept Bob's resignation

Daily Mirror, Wednesday, March 1, 1989

A dramatic offer by soccer legend Bob Paisley to resign as a Liverpool director was rejected by his colleagues last night.

But they reprimanded the former manager over the interview in yesterday's Daily Mirror about the club's problems.

He was also banned from giving any interviews in the future.

Paisley had been ordered to attend a board meeting at Anfield.

During the three and a half hour meeting, he apologised for the Mirror interview in which he assessed the problems which have sent Liverpool sliding down Division One.

Afterwards, chairman John Smith revealed that Paisley's quit offer had been turned down because of his long and distinguished association with the club.

He said: "The directors received an apology and an expression of regret from Bob Paisley for articles which appeared under his name in a national newspaper."

The young
PAISLEYS

HE KEPT A SLIDE IN HIS LIVING ROOM TO PLAY WITH THE GRANDCHILDREN THAT HE LOVED. NOW THEY ARE OLD ENOUGH TO RECOUNT THEIR OWN STORIES OF THEIR BELOVED GRANDDAD

> Alongside the newspaper cuttings in the Paisley scrapbooks are occasional letters and tributes from the fans. It's clear that these very personal messages are valued just as much as invitations to Downing Street and photos from lavish celebratory dinners. Here are a selection of those that were kept and treasured

Thanks for all you've done for the fans

Mr R. Paisley, let me say right away that you do not know me, in fact the last time I was at Anfield was in 1947 when I was stationed in Liverpool in the Royal Navy.

The reason I am writing to you is to say, in my own way a very big thank you for all that you have done for British football fans everywhere.

Whenever our national team has been savaged and made to look second rate all over the world and the critics have run us down, along came you and your team to show them how wrong they are, and enable the man on the terrace to look them in the eye and say "beat that if you can" and feel 10 feet tall and proud to be a British football fan once again.

I am sure that I am speaking for all the British fans when I say a very big, and I mean BIG thanks for what you have done for us in the past, and that your wife and yourself enjoy your retirement – the years ahead because, believe me, you have both earned it.

So at the end of the season when your team holds up the FA Cup (and I know you will) I don't think there will be a dry eye at Wembley or in front of the TV, and it could not happen to a more honest man in the whole of Britain, nay the world.

So good luck and God bless to you and your wife.

Kenneth Nash, Turnford, Herts

P.S. I say this as a former referee, and a Yorkshireman.

THE GRANDCHILDREN

Like any granddad, Bob was extremely proud of his grandchildren. Free from the responsibilities of managing Liverpool, the time that he was often denied watching his own family grow up could be devoted to a new generation of young Paisleys.

He would spend Sunday afternoons with his new young family, playing games in the house after dinner and they would become a regular fixture in his social diary.

Bob would be as proud as any of his trophy-winning Liverpool teams that his grandchildren have gone on to achieve success in their academic and professional lives.

We spoke to three of the Anfield legend's seven grandchildren on a Tuesday tea-time in their grandmother's house as they gathered to reminisce about the man they called 'Little Granddad'. Helen, 28, is a nurse at Alder Hey Hospital. She is Graham's daughter and her sister is Rachael, who is aged 24 and works as an Occupational Therapist at the Royal Liverpool Hospital. Jane is 27 and is a qualified insurance broker

Now: Jessie with (from left) Helen, Jane and Rachael

Then: The grandchildren in 1983. They are pictured on the 'indoor' slide Bob kept for them to play on

Hospital visit but Granddad got taken off to see other children

▶ **Tribute to Bob Paisley**

You have been a
credit to the game
For well over 50 years
A legend in your own lifetime
And one who showed he cares
Very few people
achieve greatness
'Opportunity' you took
with both hands
Your name is part of our history
Fond happy memories
for the fans
You are our greatest
reluctant 'hero',
A successful modest man
Our knight in shining armour
To every Liverpool fan
So have a happy retirement
'Remember', Anfield is always
your 'home',
There will always be
a welcome 'Bob'
"You'll Never Walk Alone"

**A.D. Smith
Lydiate, Merseyside**

You'd have been praised more if you were outrageous

Dear Sir (Bob),

Recently a news report suggested
you were finishing with football,
more or less.

Possibly it's false, but I still
want to tell you that nobody has
given me more pleasure than the
way you ran the team.

It all went so well – nothing
went wrong that could not be
overcome – and it was always
such glorious, attractive football!

For years I've drooled over the
wonderful skill you coaxed out of
the players and I wish you all the
very best, in your retirement, sir!

Much happiness to you and
your family – good luck to you all,
and I am one of many, many fans
who will be forever grateful to
you for your tremendous
achievements!

Perhaps if you had been a more
outrageous type of manager, you
would be more praised and
applauded now.

VIP tour: Helen with cousin Andrew at Anfield around 1980

HELEN'S STORY

Nana and granddad came to
visit me in Alder Hey when
I was having my appendix
out. They brought me a lovely
present, but I didn't get to talk to my
granddad. He got taken off to see
other children and was gone for a
couple of hours.

I remember when I visited
granddad, I would run up to him and
he would lift me high in the air. We
would be in the house before dinner
and I would climb up onto his knee.
He always had this little emblem on
his jumper and I would sit there
picking at it.

I can remember going to my Nana
when I was in primary school and
asking: 'Is my granddad famous?'
She said: "Why Helen?" and I said
that we needed someone to give out
the prizes. I didn't have a clue how
famous he really was. He was just
my granddad.

It only dawned on me when I was
getting older and other kids started
asking: 'Can I have your granddad's
autograph?'

Helen in the only surviving picture, according to son Graham, of one of the giant Manager of the Month whisky bottles. Bob rarely drank and gave away most of the many he won to friends and relatives

'I CAN REMEMBER GOING TO MY NANA WHEN I WAS IN PRIMARY SCHOOL AND ASKING: 'IS MY GRANDDAD FAMOUS?' I DIDN'T HAVE A CLUE HOW FAMOUS HE REALLY WAS. HE WAS JUST MY GRANDDAD'

You'll never be forgotten by the likes of me, Bob. Good luck to you, and yours!
God bless.

E. Hannaford
Knowle, Bristol

P.S. They aren't the same now, I'm afraid.

Best wishes and well done Bob – from across the Park

From Everton Telegraph and Shrewsbury House Youth Club, Liverpool

I don't think Evertonians, or the league and cup-winning Shrewsy O.B. Reserves, will mind a few words of admiration for the remarkable Bob Paisley.

I know he's been praised everywhere for the last few months, but he deserves it doesn't he!

Not loud-mouthed, full of himself, but quietly spoken (he reckons people will then take care to listen) and full of his team's achievements, not his own.

"We take life too lightly and sport too seriously" said one commentator, but Bob Paisley talks of laughing inside through his long football career and was always quick to joke at the over-serious TV interview question.

"No-one's allowed an ego-trip, and that starts with the chairman. It's ingrained in the players. And that's why the club remains happy", says Paisley.

And I enjoyed reading that "all Liverpool strategy takes place in the Bootroom, that snug-bar where the brew is strong tea and Shankly, Paisley and trainers Joe Fagan and Ronnie Moran have down the years always got together every day for a Coronation Street type conference of war, or gossip as they would call it."

Not that they'd say they were always right: Callaghan should have played in the '77 Cup final, and do they regret letting a certain K. Sheedy go? Or was that Paisley generosity?!

He also of course is the most successful club manager of all time. We can't win all his trophies, many of us don't support his team, but we can learn a few qualities off him. The man is more important than the trophies.

Rev. Henry Corbett

Bob Paisley – The Manager and Inspiration of LFC

On hallowed ground,
this man profound
Brought honour to the game
Lose, or win, the kindly gain
This code remained the same
"Just do your best,
that is the test"
He would say to his golden boys
"To the crowd you play,
make or break your day
but always keep your poise
Just stick to the rules,
you're no fools
as you've proved in
your special way
Altho' I retire keep
bright your fire
And strive in each
game you play
When you line up
to receive each cup
A tribute to me you pay
You've beaten the best,
you know the rest
Trophies we have galore,
but my cup you fill
Each time I thrill
To my beloved
Kop's mighty roar
So good luck boys,
we've shared great joys
Also days of sadness too
But aim still more,
you know the score
Just see what
your fate brings
So don't count me out,
without any doubt
I'll be watching
from the wings."

**Mrs V.L. Symonds,
poem written for Bob's
retirement in 1983**

RACHAEL'S STORY

Tea at Granddad's and . . . who ate all the chocolate?

And they're off: Graham and Robert join granddad for a family race!

> Letter of appreciation from a schoolteacher at St Cyril's Junior School in Netherley following Bob's visit to accept a cheque of nearly £3000 from the efforts of primary school kids around the city who ran laps at Sefton Park, in aid of Sport Aid.

Thanks for making our day special

6th January, 1987

Dear Mr Paisley,

I am writing to thank you for attending our 'Primary Aid' presentation.

Your presence on that afternoon really made it a day to remember.

The children were delighted (and many adults too) to have such a famous personality in their school. It was such an enjoyable event and your patient way with the children made it all the more enjoyable.

The press covered the event very well and this again due to your presence.

I hope you saw the Liverpool

I remember granddad having this big car, I was always excited to ride in it. On a Sunday afternoon the whole family would go round for tea at Nana and Granddad's house. My dad would be playing snooker with granddad.

Then granddad would get down on all fours and we would leap on his back pretending he was a horse. They had a rocking horse in the lounge – and a slide!

One thing that I always remember is granddad picking me up from nursery. We would go back to his house and Nana had this basket on the table with chocolate bars in. Granddad would eat them all and I can remember counting five empty wrappers in the basket.

Echo (20.12.86) and the Liverpool Star (31.12.86).

I hope too that you enjoyed yourself and that your visit to St. Cyril's was a pleasant one.

Once again, thanks for everything and may I wish you a Happy New Year.

**Your sincerely,
Joe Reilly**

Great but humble right until the last

Letter of appreciation from the brother of the caretaker of Eppleton School

May 19, 1983

Dear Mr Paisley,

A friend of mine wrote and told me of your television interview and you mentioned my brother Bowler Burns.

In all your memories of your great career, I found it touching that you could give a mention to the lowly caretaker who provided the hot water.

I can still remember him telling Bertie Rowe "that kid has a great footballing brain", when they had an inquest in the boiler house after a game.

Amazing Grace and games of 'Spanish' Snakes and Ladders

JANE'S STORY

I will always remember playing games with my granddad. My Nan had a big chess set with brass pieces. We would also play Snakes and Ladders and granddad would always count in Spanish.

Nan had an organ in the lounge and granddad would try and teach me to play Amazing Grace. He would get all frustrated when I bashed the keys. He could play by ear and was quite good at times.

When Liverpool played in Japan, grandad came back with different coloured mini Kimonos for me and my sister. He would always try and get us things from the places he visited, like a Spanish fan or a Japanese doll.

I remember when Liverpool played Everton in the Cup.

Everton defender John Gidman had gone to my school and I remember standing there, being pictured next to grandad and John and realising how special my granddad was.

Perfect fit: Jane and the others (top) with Kimonos from Tokyo.
Bob estimated the sizes he would need for his grandchildren –
and made a pretty good job of it! Above: With Jane and Helen

'WHEN LIVERPOOL PLAYED IN JAPAN,
GRANDDAD CAME BACK WITH
DIFFERENT COLOURED MINI KIMONOS
FOR ME AND MY SISTER. HE WOULD
ALWAYS TRY AND GET US THINGS
FROM THE PLACES HE VISITED, LIKE A
SPANISH FAN OR A JAPANESE DOLL'

Those midweek evening games, your duels with Jimmy Hagen with you usually on top.

Miss Boyd and Miss Davidson would visit us and want a detailed account of the match on the old Comrades football field adjoining the schoolyard.

You won't remember me, I was a sort of assistant caretaker (unpaid), but I earned many a half crown for refereeing a Saturday morning match.

Alas, the only sight I get here is of Liverpool on tele.

I shall miss you on the bench. If there is a grandstand in the sky I bet my brother and Bertie Rowe never miss a match.

I don't think, in fact I am sure your record in the game will never even be equalled, you have been a credit to the game.

Please write a book or two, as they will be worth reading.

Now when I have been in the club I have a letter to frame, I knew Bobby Paisley.

I hope you will forgive this liberty from an old man well into extra time.

God bless you, you have earned what I hope will be a long and happy retirement.

**Eddie (Bowler) Burns
Chester Hill, Sydney, Australia**

P.S. I got the half crown from Bertie. Eh it all comes back to me.

A letter of thanks from Millstead
School after Bob handed over the
keys to a new bus.

Jessie's final SNAPSHOT

DURING HIS LATTER YEARS, JESSIE COULD FINALLY SEE MORE OF HER HUSBAND. IN A REVEALING PICTURE OF THEIR HOME LIFE, SHE PRESENTED A COLOURFUL IMAGE OF THE ANFIELD MASTER

Series in Liverpool Echo by Moya Jones, February 22, 1992

Jessie spoke to the Echo as part of a series written after Bob resigned from the Liverpool board. The children, holidays, early days, DIY, gardening and Sunday church visits were among the many subjects she was happy to talk about

Jessie on Bob:

I wouldn't swap him for anybody.

I came second to football ... truly, I never resented it.

He was so committed to Liverpool. It was his job. When I met him he was a footballer. I didn't know much about what a footballer was because I'd never even been to a match.

Even in those days he'd buy a paper, even though it was only a war time game. And he might say: 'I didn't have a good game today'.

He's always honest with himself or with anybody else. It gets him into trouble sometimes but the funny thing is, he seems to be proved right in the end.

I knew football was going to be his life. So you feel, well, that's it. You've married him knowing it. You are fully aware of what's happening. You've got to lead your own independent life at the same time. It worked splendidly.

'UP UNTIL BOB RETIRED, I DID EVERY BIT OF THE GARDEN EXCEPT THE LAWN. NOW I'M TRAINING BOB. IT'S A BIT DICEY LETTING HIM DO ANY OF THE FLOWER BEDS BECAUSE HE DUG UP ALL MY MONKEY MUSK ONE MORNING, THINKING THEY WERE WEEDS!'

Half century: At a dinner for Bob's 50th year at Liverpool. Left: Helping out in the garden and (below) together in 1993 at Churchfield Court in Childwall, celebrating 10 years since Bob opened the nursing home

On bringing up the children:

Yes, I think I brought the children up. Bob had to be away so much and he was so dedicated. I used to say I only saw Bob at breakfast! When he was manager, he was seven days a week there, Sunday mornings as well. That's the nice thing since he retired – we do see him now.

On Bob having green fingers:

Up until Bob retired I did every bit of the garden except the lawn and we had someone to come and do that. Now I'm training Bob. It's a bit dicey letting him do any of the flower beds because he dug up all my Monkey Musk one morning, thinking they were weeds!

On how she first met Bob:

It's a standing joke how we met. On the midnight train to London! I always say it's better than meeting in a dance hall.

Bob had come back from abroad. He was four or five years in the army and he was at Woolwich and every weekend they used to let him travel up to Liverpool to play for the club and travel back on the Saturday midnight.

I was going on the train with a friend to London for the week and this soldier got on the train and threw his Greatcoat on my sandwiches!

I told him off. That's how we met.

On holidays:

Till Bob retired I don't think we went away together ever. You see, I was teaching and as soon as I broke up they were back at the football ground.

They'd started training. I used to take the children on holiday. Even now he's retired we travel very little.

I think he's travelled so much he's quite glad not to.

On Bob's DIY skills:

He's not a DIY enthusiast. He's very good with cement and mortar but if a fuse needs mending, one of the boys does it.

On moving in with Bob:

We were in the corner house (in houses owned by the club in Bowring Park) and it had a letter box on the ground and I remember one day seeing two little eyes looking through. I went to the door and a little boy asked: 'Can I have an autograph?' I said: 'Whose – mine?' and he said: 'No – your dad's!'

On Bob remembering anniversaries:

He remembers when I remind him! He's very good when they actually arrive but he's got to be reminded they are going to arrive. I think the family jog him about our anniversaries.

On Bob watching TV:

He's one of those who puts it on and either falls asleep or reads the paper. But he never misses a sports programme!

On Bob and football in retirement:

Well, he never misses any Liverpool games. Home and away when he became a director.
  And a lot of the reserve games. Now he has limited himself to the home games.

On the children's relationship with Bob:

They are right hero worshippers of their dad. There is no one like him to Robert, Graham and Christine. We shared the pressures. It's strange really, if anything affects Bob it affects the family. They are always concerned about him.
  It's surprising, seeing he saw so little of them as they were growing up, but they are 100 per cent behind him all the time.

Proud day: Opening the Bob Paisley Suite at Anfield in 1990

Guests of honour: At the Woolton Fete on a summer day in 1986

‘I'M THE FAMILY CHAUFFEUR THESE DAYS. AS A COMMITTED CHRISTIAN, FOR ME ONE OF THE NICE THINGS ABOUT BOB BEING RETIRED IS HAVING HIM WITH ME IN CHURCH ON SUNDAY MORNINGS. HE LIKES A GOOD SING’

On Bob going to church:

I'm the family chauffeur these days. As a committed Christian, for me one of the nice things about Bob being retired is having him with me in church on Sunday mornings. He likes a good sing and looks forward to Sunday mornings.

At first, when he could not be there very often, choir boys used to want autographs but now he's a member of the congregation they just accept him and he likes that, just to be accepted as one of the crowd.

On Bob and his grandchildren:

We see a lot of them. To be honest, I think Bob sees more of the grandchildren than he saw of his own children at that age.

He seemed to be away the whole time. I remember when we were doing This Is Your Life about 15 years ago the man saying to Graham 'What kind of parent was your father?' and Graham said: 'My dad didn't bring us up. My mum brought us up.'

Celebrity opening: At Batley's Wholesale Market in July, 1987

The Paisley LEGACY

IN 1996, ANFIELD MOURNED THE PASSING OF THEIR MOST SUCCESSFUL MANAGER. BUT HIS ACHIEVEMENTS HAD GIVEN LIFE TO AN 'IMPOSSIBLE' DREAM FOR FUTURE GENERATIONS

Fans gathered at Anfield on Valentine's Day, 1996, as news of Bob Paisley's death in a Liverpool nursing home broke. It seemed like the wise old man of Liverpool would be around forever. If Paisley was gone, though, he could rest in peace knowing his name – and his legacy – would live on

Goodbye Bob

Liverpool Echo, February 14, 1996

Liverpool Football Club chief executive Peter Robinson said today: "We are all very sorry to hear of Bob's death and our thoughts go out to his wife and family.

"He spent a lifetime in the service of the club and his record is unprecedented.

"Many people, not only from Liverpool, will mourn his passing because he was a most popular figure in the football world."

Former Liverpool captain Emlyn Hughes, who skippered Paisley's team to their finest hour in Rome in 1977 said: "He was a super fella. He was Liverpool through and through. He led the club to unprecedented success. That will never be matched by any manager in Britain."

Jessie and sons at bedside as battling Bob loses his fight in nursing home

Thanks, Bob: Flowers and scarves pay tribute to the passing of a Liverpool legend

Liverpool Echo, Wednesday, February 14, 1996

Crowds started to gather at Anfield this afternoon as news of the death of one of the club's gfreatest heroes spread.

Floral tributes were paid to Bob Paisley as lifelong fans arrived at the ground.

Taxi driver Ron Willingham said: "I knew Bob through a Sunday team I played in and he was a real gent.

"He always had time for you – for anyone – and he was a great ambassador for the club and for football as a whole.

"He was respected by all – the players, the fans, everyone involved in the game."

Liverpool-born William Purcell, visiting Anfield from his present home in Blackpool, was shattered by the news.

He said: "He was a great man. I remember him very vividly as a player and manager and it is a terrible loss to the club.

"This city has lost two great men in a week – Bob and Archbishop Worlock."

Edie McNaughton, of Walton, added: "I'm in my 60s and he was always such a hero. Not just for the club but because he seemed like a nice man as well. It is a real shame."

Fan Dave Porter, 25, said: "It is really sad."

Liverpool Echo February 14, 1996

Liverpool's Anfield legend Bob Paisley died today. The former Liverpool FC manager passed away peacefully at the Arncliffe Court Nursing Home, Halewood, at 9.30am, following a long illness.

His wife, Jessie, was at his bedside and his sons, Graham and Robert, arrived shortly after he died.

Mr Paisley was 77 and had been suffering from Alzheimer's Disease.

He spent his last 14 months at the nursing home where he and his family had become very popular.

Mr Paisley OBE devoted his working life to Liverpool FC and became the country's most successful manager during his nine years at the helm. He went on to become a director at the club after retiring in 1983.

Tributes poured in this afternoon for the man who was born in the Durham mining ▶

Bob was suffering – but he was still the same character he always was

➤ village of Hetton-le-Hole but who went on to have such a massive impact on Merseyside and world football.

A relative, who declined to be named, said: "Bob was finally released from his pain this morning.

Liverpool players will wear black armbands when they take on Shrewsbury in the FA Cup on Sunday. Mr Paisley leaves a wife, two sons, one daughter, Christine and several grandchildren.

"Bob had long been suffering from Alzheimer's Disease but he was still the fearsome character he always was," the relative added.

"He will be very sadly missed by the family and I am sure the whole of Liverpool will be in mourning for this great man."

Gail Hall, matron of the Arncliffe Court Nursing Home, said: "Mr Paisley had been poorly for quite some time.

"He finally died of complications resulting from the Alzheimer's Disease. He was very popular here, as were his whole family, and we are very sad."

Respect: Players wear armbands before their FA Cup tie against Shrewsbury

Messages of support flood in for family

February 15, 1996
Liverpool Echo

The funeral of Liverpool football legend Bob Paisley will take place next Wednesday.

Many fans and admirers are expected to attend the ex-Reds manager's local church in Woolton to pay their last respects.

Son Robert said today: "We know that many will want to pay their respects to dad.

"People are usually very sensitive to such events and although the funeral is not just for family only I am sure they will be equally sensitive on this occasion."

Robert also spoke of how touched the family had been by an avalanche of messages of support from friends and colleagues from the football world and beyond.

His father passed away yesterday morning at a Halewood nursing home, with wife Jessie by his side.

Robert said: "My mum had quite a few phone calls last night and I think they have helped her cope. But she doesn't really want a lot of fuss.

"My dad had been ill for a while so it wasn't really unexpected but it's still a ▶

The Liverpool Echo: Told how
fans sent 'avalanche' of letters

I knew what would happen ... I just feel hollow now – Jessie

❯ shock you can't quite prepare yourself for.

"We're a fairly close family and my brother is on his way home to Liverpool and being close should help us during such a difficult time."

Jessie Paisley thanked the staff at the Arncliffe Court Nursing Home who had cared for her husband so well during the illness.

She said: "Bob had been suffering from Alzheimer's Disease and had been in the nursing home for the past 14 months.

"I knew what was about to happen because Bob's condition had worsened. I just feel hollow now.

"So many people have been in touch, including Bob's football colleagues and friends not connected with the sport."

National Heritage Secretary Virginia Bottomley said: "Bob Paisley was one of the greatest managers in English football."

Harry Rimmer, leader of Liverpool City Council, added: "There were those who said Bill Shankly was an impossible act to follow but they had not reckoned with Bob Paisley.

"He brought unprecedented success and prestige to Liverpool Football Club and will be remembered as a man of extraordinary modesty and dignity."

A Commons motion paying tribute to Paisley and already signed by many MPs of all parties has been tabled by Riverside Labour MP Bob Parry.

The funeral will be held at noon next Wednesday at St. Peter's Church in Woolton, the church Mr Paisley regularly attended with his wife before his illness.

Jessie Paisley has asked for family flowers only, with donations instead going to help the rebuilding of the church centre at St. Peter's.

Tribute: Liverpool manager in 1996 Roy Evans pays his own respects

Anfield's humble hero

Tributes have poured into Liverpool FC from all over the world following the sad death of Anfield legend Bob Paisley at the age of 77 after a long illness.

It is a loss which has united football fans of all loyalties. Right across the city, Reds and Blues have come together to pay their respects to a great man of football.

As a manager he had an unprecedented record of achievements – 19 trophies in nine seasons including no fewer than six League titles and three European Cups.

As a member of the Anfield "family" he had a unique record of service – more than 50 years as a player, member of the backroom team, manager – picking up the reins from another Anfield legend, Bill Shankly – and a director.

As manager it was a tough act to follow. Yet Bob Paisley went on to better even the great Shankly's record.

Perhaps it was because of his quiet personality that his achievements were often overlooked whenever football legends were discussed. But Bob Paisley was, without question, in a class of his own. He had an eminent place in any soccer Hall of Fame.

He was never one of football's flamboyant managers; never one who sought or enjoyed the spotlight of publicity.

He was the quiet personality who preferred to get on with his job without fuss and let the players' achievements on the pitch do the talking.

The success he brought to Liverpool FC – and the manner of that success through football of an outstanding quality – will long be remembered and savoured by the many thousands who saw Liverpool in those momentous years.

Bob Paisley leaves a legacy of football greatness, the like of which the game may never see again.

Yet it is a wonderful tribute to this adopted son of Liverpool that he will equally be remembered for the man he was – humble and unassuming in the spotlight of greatness, ever caring and concerned for all those about him.

Our thought and sympathy are with Mr Paisley's widow Jessie and her family with the hope that they will be greatly comforted by the knowledge that he was held in such high respect and genuine affection by so many people.

**Liverpool Echo Comment,
February 15, 1996**

Bye Bye Bob

Daily Star,
February 22, 1996

Playing stars of almost half a century ago were there, alongside today's leading lights of the game.

But it was the tears of the youngster that illustrated the lasting memory of a man unchanged by success – described by local vicar Canon John Roberts as always a "quiet, self-effacing, unassuming Geordie."

He was, said Mr Roberts, totally unspoiled by success.

A truly extraordinary "ordinary" man.

He added: "There will be something missing from the lives of most people in football because Bob is not here."

Salute To Uncle Bob

Daily Mirror,
February 22, 1996

There may have been some of the biggest names in the game paying their last respects at his local church, St. Peter's in Woolton, and they may have honoured him under the same leaded roof where John Lennon and Paul McCartney practised as The Quarry Men before they became Beatles.

But that was the only connection with superstardom, the only giveaway that Bob Paisley, OBE, the former bricklayer from Hetton-le-Hole, Co. Durham, had found world-wide fame as player and boss.

He shied away from that image. He was a modest genius at his happiest talking football in the Anfield Boot-room or watching TV at home with Jessie, his wife of nearly 50 years.

Four pall-bearers carried the dark wood coffin, which was topped fittingly with a wreath of red and white flowers, up the slope to the church entrance.

Already, packed inside, were his footballing friends.

'A TEAM FROM FOOTBALL'S WHO'S WHO WITH ONE NAME ON THEIR MIND ON A DAY WHEN TOO MANY TEARS WERE RULED OFFSIDE. INSTEAD THERE WERE SMILES WHEN A SNAPSHOT ALBUM OF BOB'S CELEBRATED LIFE WAS CONJURED UP'

There were legends spanning 50 glorious years of football.

Some had played with him. Many against. But they were all united in saying goodbye to the greatest.

Kenny Dalglish, Roy Evans, Graeme Souness, Ray Clemence, Alan Hansen, Ian Rush, Bruce Grobbelaar, Steve McMahon, Phil Thompson, Steve Nicol, Tommy Smith, Joe Fagan, Roger Hunt, Emlyn Hughes and Ian Callaghan.

All from the Anfield culture club and joined by Lawrie McMenemy, Tommy Docherty, Nat Lofthouse, Jimmy Armfield and Sir Bobby Charlton.

A team from football's Who's Who with one name on their mind and in their thoughts on a day when too many tears were ruled offside.

Instead there were smiles when an imaginary snapshot album of Bob's celebrated life was conjured up by Canon John Roberts.

He spoke of the brickie who served a seven-year apprenticeship and even when as the boss of champions Liverpool had revelled in building patios and garages for his friends and neighbours.

Of Bob the soldier, who rode aboard a tank to help liberate Rome in the Second World War.

And who said later when Liverpool played there in a European Cup final: "The last time I was here 33 years ago I captured the city."

Canon Roberts talked about Bob the bridegroom, who was stationed at Woolwich Arsenal during the war and bumped into Jessie on a train travelling north.

Bob threw his trenchcoat over her sandwich basket by accident in the carriage and a year after the war they married.

Then there was Bob the family man.

The father and granddad who read the kids Mister Men books and gave piggy-backs across the lounge floor.

'Hang on – you serve the petrol and I'll pick the team!'

He also played them at every game imaginable – and would never allow them to win.

We heard about Bob the footballer who won every honour known to man.

But even at the height of his glory he would never look down on anyone from his dizzy perch.

He lived in the same home and drove the same little Ford car.

On his way to training, he would stop off at the Wheatsheaf Garage and mix with his kind of people – the mechanics, the petrol pump attendants.

And he'd answer the phone, make tea and pick out the horses for a few bob each-way bet.

He would talk endlessly about football, with the garage lads daring to advise him on team selection.

"Hang on," he'd say. "You serve the petrol and leave me to pick the team."

Finally, we were told about Bob the Royal Approval. Of the day the Queen handed over the OBE to the Liverpool boss.

Her Majesty noted that he'd had a lot of success in football to which Bob, suffering amid a mini-slump at Anfield, replied: "You haven't been reading the newspapers in the last couple of months."

'WE HEARD ABOUT BOB THE FOOTBALLER WHO WON EVERY HONOUR KNOWN TO MAN. BUT EVEN AT THE HEIGHT OF HIS GLORY HE WOULD NEVER LOOK DOWN ON ANYONE FROM HIS DIZZY PERCH. HE LIVED IN THE SAME HOME AND DROVE THE SAME LITTLE FORD CAR'

From left: Steve Nicol, Ian Rush, Alan Hansen; Roy Evans. Opposite: Graeme Souness; Bruce Grobbelaar and David Moores

We'll never forget the man called 'Dougie'

Bob either saw I had something to offer on the coaching side – or that I couldn't play! He encouraged me to go into coaching. Bob, Joe Fagan and Ronnie Moran were always helping me. They saw me as a 25-year-old lad coaching a team and I could always go to them if I had a problem.

On occasions I would tell Bob I wasn't sure of something and he'd tell me I wasn't the only one. I learned that anyone who thinks they know everything about football is kidding you.

We had an affectionate nickname for Bob. There was a guy in Wolverhampton called Dougie somebody. I can't remember his name.

But Bob could never remember it, so each time he referred to him he called him 'Dougie Do-ins'. That's how the name Dougie stuck with Bob. It was an affectionate name.

Bob wasn't a great communicator, especially in his early days. What he said was quite fragmented sometimes, but he always managed to get his point across.

What he told people was so simple it could be said in one or two words. His results showed that he could make a point or two!

I never thought Shanks would retire. I don't think Bob particularly wanted the job, but thought: 'If I don't take it, who will they give it to, and what about the lads in the jobs?'

It doesn't surprise me what Bob achieved because he worked with Shanks and had Joe and Ronnie to lean on.

For me, the first manager was Shanks. I thought that the next one had to be like him, but it doesn't have to be that way.

It's like selling a player. We thought that after Terry McDermott or Kevin Keegan went we needed other players exactly like them, but we didn't.

Bob could never be another 'Shanks.' Nor did he want to be. But he went about his job well, as the number of trophies shows.

Bob took individuals and made them better. But the biggest thing that's been preached here is that you get your best results from team performances.

Bob would have a go at players if he thought it necessary. He could lose his temper and tear into us.

Or if he didn't, he would load the bullets for others to fire, as 'Shanks' did.

Football management is a partnership. It's not about the manager alone.

Liverpool boss Roy Evans

Common sense was Bob's strength

Bob won't be remembered for his highly sophisticated tactical analysis of the game. He'll be remembered for plain common sense.

There is so much said nowadays about tactics. People watch three or four videos of opponents before they play them. Bob wasn't into that. I was privileged over the years to be his spy in Europe.

All he wanted from me was information on set-plays and strengths and weaknesses.

He didn't want reams of paper and diagrams because he recognised he had good players and that every game was different, anyway.

Bob had inherited the Bill Shankly philosophy that football is a simple game.

I've probably had the confidence of Shankly, Bob Paisley, Joe Fagan, Kenny Dalglish, Graeme Souness and Roy Evans more than anybody – but perhaps none more so than Bob. We had a very close relationship. I will remember him as a very unassuming man. No way was he ever a self-publicist. He didn't want to project himself as many other people did. If anyone has spoken with more knowledge than Bob about football, then I never met them.

Tom Saunders

Family man with a true sense of sporting values

He headed the finest backroom staff any club could have. He was supported by Joe Fagan, Ronnie Moran and Roy Evans, all experts like himself all quiet men who just got on with the job and never shouted the odds.

Paisley was the key man as they created the sense of family, of togetherness, which made Liverpool a lasting legend in the game. Behind all this was his personal life, his own family. His loved ones gave him constant support, inspired and nurtured by his devoted wife Jessie.

A Liverpool Primary School teacher, who loved her husband, her children, the church and gardening which formed the basis of the Paisley lifestyle, she did not become involved in football matters. That was Bob's separate life but the warmth and sanctity of his home was always there for him in full measure.

He was always shy with non-football people. He was not a conversationalist. Before my retirement I used to help Bob prepare speeches he had to make from time to time. He had dozens of invitations to speak and accepted some of them.

We arrived at a speaking formula which seemed to pay off. I prepared a brief summing up of life at Liverpool Football Club with which Bob opened his talk.

It only lasted a few minutes and then came the questions. They came thick and fast and he was good at answering them where he would have been worried about a speech.

Bob Paisley became a great friend of mine. He was so honest, so straight and genuine in a sporting world very short of men of real character like him.

**Liverpool Echo's
Michael Charters**

Bob was a great bloke to work with. When I joined the club he was already here and I was lucky enough to play a few games with him in the early '50s.

It's been mentioned that it was easy for Bob because he was at Liverpool and he had all those good players.

But nowadays there is a lot of money and good players around, so why can't other clubs achieve the same as Bob did?

The players Bob bought were available to other clubs. There was nothing to stop them trying to buy them.

Bob had an eye for players. This was one of his great strengths. He knew a player's strength and he knew a player's weakness.

One player's strength would take care of another's weakness. Bob had the ability to blend a team together.

If you get together a squad of players who are willing to help each other out when things aren't going well, then you'll win things.

This is why we won so many trophies over the years. But players have got to be handled the right way and Bob was able to do that.

Years ago we tried playing three at the back in one of our pre-season matches – long before it came into the English game. But Bob saw our players weren't doing it so we didn't play that way. Other managers would have forced their team to play like that.

It's all about players playing to strengths. Bob wouldn't ask a player to do something which wasn't in his nature.

People tell me that the game has changed, but it hasn't.

Bob would still be the same now. You can't change people like that.

Ronnie Moran

'HE HEADED THE FINEST BACKROOM STAFF ANY CLUB COULD HAVE. PAISLEY WAS THE KEY MAN AS THEY CREATED A SENSE OF TOGETHERNESS. BEHIND ALL THIS WAS HIS OWN FAMILY . . . HIS LOVED ONES WHO GAVE HIM CONSTANT SUPPORT'

PAISLEY'S NAME LIVES ON

Liverpool fans scale the Paisley Gates at Anfield hours after the Reds had won the Champions League final in Istanbul in May, 2005. The famous gates were built in 1999, a year after Paisley's death – a fitting reminder of his achievements – especially his three European Cups which are incorporated into their design

April, 1999

The Paisley Gates

The Paisley Gates were erected on Thursday, April 8, 1999, and now stand proudly in front of The Kop at Anfield.

Jessie and Bob's family liaised closely with the architects to design the gates which, as well as celebrating Bob's three European Cups, also acknowledge his home town.

The image of a steam engine on a crest adorning one of the gates is symbolic of Hetton-le-Hole and the role that the small North-East village played in the industrial revolution. On the facing gate is a Liverbird – acknowledging not just the club but also Bob's love of his adopted city.

Sitting either side of the gates are two plaques which pay tribute to the honours he won at Anfield.

Fittingly, Jessie was present when the gates were unveiled and told the Liverpool Echo: "If this was an Oscar ceremony I would be expected to fling my arms around, burst into tears and say Bob didn't deserve it.

"But although the tears aren't far away, I'm not going to say that. If you ask me if Bob deserved it, I say 'Yes, 100 per cent' ".

She added: "I may be putting my foot in it but I believe the European Cup was much harder to win than now. For Bob to win it three times was the jewel in the crown."

Liverpool chairman David Moores said: "We offer our thanks to Bob for so many memories that we cherish."

'IF THIS WAS AN OSCAR CEREMONY I WOULD BE EXPECTED TO FLING MY ARMS AROUND, BURST INTO TEARS AND SAY BOB DIDN'T DESERVE IT. BUT ALTHOUGH THE TEARS AREN'T FAR AWAY, I'M NOT GOING TO SAY THAT. IF YOU ASK ME IF BOB DESERVED IT, I SAY 'YES, 100 PER CENT''

BOB PAISLEY O.B.E.

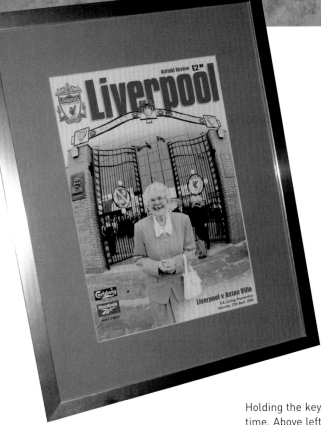

Holding the key: Jessie opens the Paisley Gates for the first time. Above left: The front page of the matchday programme and (top) the two plaques which sit either side of the gates

**February 22, 2001
Liverpool v AS Roma,
UEFA Cup, fourth round:**
Paisley Tribute Night

Liverpool fans love celebrating
the heroes of their illustrious
past and so it was when Liverpool
played host to AS Roma in
February, 2001.

The Reds had won the first leg of
their fourth round tie 2-0 thanks to
a famous Michael Owen double in
Italy and Anfield was braced for
another historic European night.

To add to the occasion, the club
officially dubbed the game a Paisley
Flag Day, with supporters
encouraged to salute their former
boss. Kopites responded in their
usual style and the Reds marched
on – despite a 1-0 setback – to
claim the trophy in a famous treble
campaign.

Paisley would have been proud.

A Kop mosaic saluting Bob Paisley's European Cup triumphs from the Liverpool v AS Roma UEFA Cup game in 2001

Never forgotten: A banner in the Kop in 1999. Opposite left: Paisley and Rome '77 Flag Day flyers

March 13, 2007

The Sir Bob Campaign

40,000 demand a Paisley knighthood

icliverpool.com

Thousands sign e-petition calling for Bob knighthood

The European Cup count between Britain's most successful managers is stacked in Paisley's favour as this Kop banner from the Liverpool v Manchester United Premiership clash at Anfield in March, 2007 is happy to point out

A petition calling for a posthumous knighthood for legendary Liverpool manager Bob Paisley closes today.

By last night, nearly 40,000 fans had registered their vote on the Downing Street e-petition. The Prime Minister has already promised to consider an award, even if a full-blown knighthood proves constitutionally impossible.

A last minute surge in support will make it impossible for ministers to shelve that commitment.

The petition was lodged by veteran fan Ian Little and it is now in the top five of the 4,800 on the No 10 website.

The Government previously ignored a similar plea from another fan, Dennis Dutton of Dingle, who wrote to No 10 in 2004. Constitutional experts have been agonising over whether a posthumous knighthood is possible.

If you compare like with like, Dad is a startling omission

By Graham Paisley

**The Sir Bob
Campaign**

**Son joins Paisley
honour call**

icliverpool.com

My mum, 'Lady' Jessie Paisley, who is 91, is thrilled by the petition. Obviously I'm somewhat biased but to me, my Dad's achievements are unsurpassed in British and European football.

I know he would have deflected any praise from himself and given credit to the team but his nine-year management of the club was unsurpassed. The three European Cups he won were the real jewels in the crown.

Many managers today would like just a fraction of the honours that he won.

People are still coming to Liverpool because they watched them as a child.

My Dad is part of Liverpool's history and it is testament to his success that this petition has got under way.

Such a recognition has been suggested before and I think, if you compare like with like, my father is a startling omission. I would particularly like it for my mum, who supported my Dad through his 50 years here at Liverpool. It would be a fitting tribute.

Despite 40,000 signing the e-petition, including current and former Liverpool players, Paisley was again denied a knighthood. Downing Street returned its verdict in April 2007 . . .

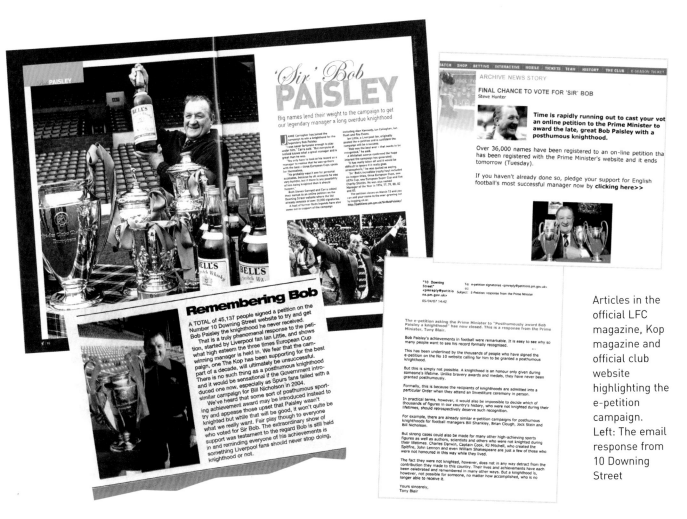

'Bob Paisley's achievements in football were remarkable. It is easy to see why so many people want to see his record formally recognised. But this is simply not possible. A knighthood is an honour only given during someone's lifetime. Unlike bravery awards and medals, they have never been granted posthumously. In practical terms, it would also be impossible to decide which of thousands of figures in our country's history, who were not knighted during their lifetimes, should retrospectively deserve such recognition'

Articles in the official LFC magazine, Kop magazine and official club website highlighting the e-petition campaign. Left: The email response from 10 Downing Street

'Bob Paisley's achievements in football were remarkable. It is easy to see why so many people want to see his record formally recognised. But this is simply not possible. A knighthood is an honour only given during someone's lifetime. Unlike bravery awards and medals, they have never been granted posthumously. In practical terms, it would also be impossible to decide which of thousands of figures in our country's history, who were not knighted during their lifetimes, should retrospectively deserve such recognition'

– Prime Minister Tony Blair, April 2007

'I'm not surprised by the decision but obviously it's disappointing. It just wasn't to be. I think if he was alive in the present political climate, my Dad would be given a knighthood. He would compare with anyone today in football. I think some people today would swap their knighthoods for one of the European Cups my Dad won with Liverpool. I have spoken to my mum about it and she accepts it and it was what we all thought would happen. My mum thinks it should have been some time ago after the first or second European Cup win when he should have been knighted. I'm sure my dad would smile. He always loved to win things. He didn't have a store for the medals to go on show. It was just the winning that counted'

– Graham Paisley's response, April 2007

1. War medals, including (far left) the Star of Africa and (second from right) the Star of Italy
2. Champions League plaque celebrating 50 years of European football, presented to family on Anfield pitch, 2005. 3. Eric Morecambe Memorial Award 1984-85. 4. Royal Doulton figure of St George awarded by press to mark retirement, 1983. 5. 1980 Charity Shield medal. 6. The Sportsman's Award of the Month for May, 1977. 7&13. 1977 European Cup winner's medal. 8. First Division winner's medal 1975-76. 9. Plate from Maccabi Tel Aviv, Israel. 10. Glass vase presented by Northern Ireland Supporters Club, Newtownards. 11. Box holding war medals sent to former address

1. Mounted glass football awarded to LFC directors after 1985/86 FA Cup and League Double. 2. Plaque from the Al Nasr Club in Dubai, presented in 1979. 3. Crystal bowl presented by Waterford branch of Liverpool Supporters Club on anniversary of 40th year at Liverpool, 1979. 4. Plate received from Athletic Bilbao. 5. Silver box presented by Borussia Dortmund. 6. Army patches. 7. FA Amateur Cup winner's medal, won playing for Bishop Auckland, 1938-39. 8. Liverpool-Israel plaque, 1979. 9. One of many Manager of the Year silver trays, awarded by Bell's Whisky. 10. Order of the British Empire medal (OBE), awarded in 1977. 11. National dolls brought from Europe for daughter Christine. 12. Commemorative club plate, produced in 1983. 13. Cup presented by Dundalk Football Club on occasion of European Cup first round, first leg tie, September 14, 1982

10

11

8

6

7

9

1. North East Football Writers Association tribute, 1982. 2. Glass vase from Nottingham Forest. 3. Daily Star Gold award, 1982. 4. Paisley Gates model presented to family by Danbury Mint. 5. International Club Achievement Award. 6. Dundalk v Liverpool European Cup plaque, 1982. 7. Liverpool Publicity Association medal. 8. LFC Supporters Club plaque in honour of 1966 title. 9. Gift from Malta Liverpool Supporters Club, Gozo branch. 10. Football League of Ireland v Liverpool plate from August, 1978. 11. Manager of the Year trophy, 1979

1

2

5

Presented to BOB PAISLEY
by THE BOARD
to mark his retirement
as Manager of
LIVERPOOL F.C.
JT & CO. LTD.

UR CUP FINAL
MARCH 1983
VERPOOL 2
ESTER UNITED

FINAL

PARIS, 27 DE MAYO 1981

DECEMBER 13th.,
1981
NATIONAL STADIUM
TOKYO JAPAN
PRESENTED
By
TOYOTA

NATIONAL FOOTBALL MUSEUM
HALL OF FAME
INAUGURAL INDUCTEE

KEY TO PAISLE
OPENED 8th J

3

4

1. Glass decanter presented by Tottenham Hotspur Football Club to mark 1983 retirement. 2. Glass Milk Cup final trophy celebrating 2-0 victory over Manchester United in 1983. 3. Plate produced in honour of the 1981 European Cup final v Real Madrid in Paris. 4. 1981 World Club Championship medal. 5. Trophy presented to mark induction into National Football Museum Hall of Fame. 6. Key presented at opening of Paisley Gates, 1999. 7. Another Daily Star Gold Award medal. 8. BAE model presented after prize presentation, 1984. 9. Watercolour painting, one of a number by Jim Rehill. 10. 1978 Club Brugges v Liverpool European Cup final trophy. 11. 1978 Super Cup trophy. 12. First Division championship medal 1979-80. 13. Toyota Cup medal

THE OLD GUNNER WINS AGAIN

SECOND BATTLE OF SPION KOP

AGHEILA MARCH 1941 ... THE SIGNAL WAS "TWO SHOTS" (THAT WAS A LONG CAMPAIGN TOO)

ANFIELD MAY 1982 ... THE SIGNAL WAS "THREE POINTS"

N°1 (LIVERPOOL) BATTERY

"PAISLEY'S OWN"

PRESENTED TO BOB PAISLEY ESQ. O.B.E. BY THE APPRENTICES OF B.AE. CHESTER ON THE OCCASION OF PRIZE PRESENTATION 1984.

TOYOTA EUROPEAN/SOUTH AMERICAN CUP

...ale Europabeker Landskampioenen ...lub Brugge K.V. - Liverpool F.C. Wembley 10 mei 1978

SUPER-CUP R.S.C. ANDERLECHT 4-12-1978

1

CITY OF NEWCASTLE UPON TYNE

LUNCHEON AT THE OFFICAL OPENING OF THE

TWENTY-FIRST TYNESIDE SUMMER EXHIBITION

by
MR BOB PAISLEY
1982/1983 Football League Manager of the Year
as
Manager of Liverpool AFC The League Champions

on
TUESDAY 26th JULY 1983

4

Barclays Bank PLC

Mr Owen Rout, Executive Director
requests the pleasure of the company of

Mr Bob Paisley

at the
Barclays Bank Managers Awards Buffet Luncheon
on Friday, 19th May, 1989
in Great Hall
at 54 Lombard Street, London EC3

R.S.V.P. (card enclosed)
John Wall   12.30 pm for 1 pm
Barclays Bank PLC
Fleetway House
25 Farringdon Street   Entrance to Great Hall
London EC4A 4LT   17 Gracechurch Street

5

BISHOP AUCKLAND F.C.

KINGS WAY GROUND
BISHOP AUCKLAND

SOUVENIR PROGRAMME
30p

1886   1986

BISHOP AUCKLAND TEAM 1986

BISHOP AUCKLAND
VS
LIVERPOOL

CENTENARY GAME

WEDNESDAY
19th November
1986

7.30 pm

DRYBROUGHS NORTHERN LEAGUE

BISHOP AUCKLAND TEAM 1939
with Bob Paisley front row - far right, immediately
behind him is the present Club Treasurer, Harry Young

2

LANCASHIRE
County Cricket Club
TEST CENTENARY APPEAL 1984

One Hundred Years of Test Cricket at
Old Trafford
1884 England v Australia 10-12th July
1984 England v West Indies 26-31st July
Cornhill Insurance Test Series

Sportsmans' Dinner

in the
TRAFFORD SUITE, OLD TRAFFORD
on
Thursday, 21st June, 1984

3

THE FOOTBALL ASSOCIATION

F.A. CHARITY SHIELD MATCH

LIVERPOOL V MANCHESTER UNITED

to be played at
WEMBLEY STADIUM, WEMBLEY
SATURDAY 20th AUGUST 1983

Kick-off 3.00 p.m.

Admit Bearer to Stadium and to
THE ROYAL BOX
(Enter At Stadium Restaurant)

The Chairman and Trustees of
The Monks Ferry Training Trust

have pleasure in inviting

Mr & Mrs R. Paisley

to the
Monks Ferry Training Workshop
Church Street, Birkenhead
on Thursday 10th December 1987 at 9.45 a.m.

on the occasion of a visit by
His Royal Highness the Prince of Wales, KG, KT, PC, GCB

R.S.V.P. – CHIEF EXECUTIVE

Guests must produce this invitation to Security on arrival

6

FOOTBALL WRITERS' ASSOCIATION

DINNER PARTY

with
BOB PAISLEY, O.B.E.
on
Sunday, 29th January, 1984
at

THE SAVOY
Strand, London, W.C.2
(River Entrance)

Reception: 7 p.m.
Dinner: 8 p.m.   BLACK TIE
Dancing

7

THE OFFICE OF
WHO'S WHO
35 · BEDFORD ROW · LONDON · WC1R 4JH

24 September 1982

Robert Paisley, Esq., OBE,

Dear Sir,

We have noted in the press that you intend
to retire at the end of this season. We have amended your
entry to read Manager, Liverpool Football Club, 1974 –
May 1983. Please do not trouble to reply if this is
correct; Who's Who 1983 is published at the end of
March 1983.

Yours faithfully,   CR-C

A. & C. Black Ltd.

Various invitations and souvenirs from matches, luncheons,
awards dinners and charity visits collected over the years:

1. Programme to Tyneside Summer Exhibition officially opened
by Bob Paisley. 2. Sportsman's dinner invitation. 3. Charity
Shield ticket for Royal Box, 1983. 4. Awards buffet invitation.
5. Bishop Auckland centenary match programme. 6. Football
Writers Association invitation. 7. Who's Who's book letter.
8. International Garden Festival invitation to official opening by
The Queen. 9. Private box ticket to 1986 FA Cup final Liverpool v
Everton at Wembley. 10. Invitation to dinner in honour of the
Indian Cricket Team. 11. Awards dinner invitation. 12&18.
Freedom of the City of Liverpool souvenirs. 13. Match
programme from Bob's last game in charge of Liverpool.
14&15. Football Writers Association 1982 souvenirs. 16. Football
Writers Association tribute, 1984. 17. Savoy Hotel invitation to
Men of Year Luncheon. 19. Charity certificate awarded to Bob.
20. Awards presentation invitation

8

International Garden Festival 1984

Leslie C. Young CBE, DL,
Chairman of the Merseyside Development Corporation
and
Lord Aberconway, Commissioner General
request the pleasure of the company of

Mr. B. Paisley and Guest

at the official opening of the Festival by

Her Majesty The Queen

accompanied by

His Royal Highness The Duke of Edinburgh

on the morning of Wednesday 2nd May 1984

9

WEMBLEY STADIUM

Football Association
Challenge Cup Final Tie
SAT., 10 MAY, 1986
KICK-OFF 3.00 p.m.
YOU ARE ADVISED TO TAKE UP
YOUR POSITION BY 2.30 p.m.
1. This ticket is not transferable. 2. This counterfoil must be retained for at least 6 months.

NORTH STAND PRIVATE BOX
£25.00

TO BE RETAINED

ISSUED SUBJECT TO THE
CONDITIONS ON BACK

Admit at Banqueting
Hall Entrance
between E & F
Turntiles thence
by Private Staircase

ROW
D
SEAT
7

10

Dr SHIV PANDE J.P.
General Secretary

Indo-British Association
Northern Branch

Requests the pleasure of the Company of

Mr. & Mrs. R. Paisley

at

Reception Dinner

to honour

SUNIL GAVASKAR and the members of THE INDIAN CRICKET TEAM
(Winners of World Cup 1983 & Asia Cup 1984)
and to celebrate the Centenary Year of
Lancashire County Cricket Club, Old Trafford, Manchester
on Tuesday 17th July 1984
at Formby Suite, Britannia Adelphi Hotel, Lime Street, Liverpool L3 5UL

Reception — 8.00pm
Dinner — 8.30pm

Dress - Lounge Suit

Parking facilities available
in Mount Pleasant Car Park

RSVP Iba Northern Branch, 14 North View, Liverpool L7 8TS

051-709 3779/709 3324

Admittance by
this ticket only

iba

In Honour of Liverpool Football Club

The Chairman of Liverpool City Council
(Councillor Hugh Dalton)

requests the pleasure of the company of

Mr. & Mrs. R. Paisley

on Monday, 28th July, 1986

at the Town Hall

at a Dinner

R.S.V.P.
Town Hall,
Liverpool L2 3SW
Tel: 236 5181

11

LIVERPOOL PUBLICITY ASSOCIATION

GOLD MEDAL
AWARD
LUNCHEON

Liverpool Moat House
Friday
12th May 1989
12.15 for 12.45 p.m.

V.I.P.

15

FOOTBALL WRITERS' ASSOCIATION
(North East Branch)
and
VAUX BREWERIES
present
'A TRIBUTE TO BOB PAISLEY'
at their
third annual dinner
in the
THREE TUNS HOTEL, DURHAM
Sunday, May 9th, 1982
7.00 for 7.30p.m.
Tickets £12·50   Dinner Jacket

12

Conferment of the
HONORARY FREEDOM
· of the ·
CITY of LIVERPOOL
1983

· upon ·

ROBERT PAISLEY OBE

16

FOOTBALL WRITERS' ASSOCIATION

Tribute to

BOB PAISLEY, O.B.E.

January 29th, 1984

14

FOOTBALL WRITERS' ASSOCIATION
(North East Branch)
and
VAUX BREWERIES
Present a tribute to

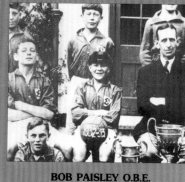

BOB PAISLEY O.B.E.

at the
THREE TUNS HOTEL, DURHAM

Sunday, May 9th, 1982

17

The Royal Association for Disability and Rehabilitation

Admittance card to the

MEN OF THE YEAR LUNCHEON

Sponsored by Access

Savoy Hotel, 9th November 1983

Reception: River Room 12.15 p.m.
Luncheon: Lancaster Room 1 p.m.

Access

18

Conferment of the Honorary Freedom of the
City of Liverpool

upon

Mr. Robert Paisley, O.B.E.

Ceremony and Reception

Mountford Hall, Students' Union Building, Liverpool University

Wednesday, 23rd November, 1983 at 4.30 p.m.

Please use Mount Pleasant Entrance

Dress: Lounge Suit

ADMIT ONE PERSON
Guests should be seated by 4.15 p.m.
Doors open 3.45 p.m.

19

The Friends of Halewood Children's Home

THE FRIENDS COMMITTEE OF THE
HALEWOOD CHILDRENS HOME
PRESENTS
THIS CERTIFICATE OF APPRECIATION
TO

Mr Bob Paisley

Hereby recording its full appreciation
and gratitude for the help and support
given to them in furthering the
objects ...

13

Watford

TODAY'S MATCH SPONSORS
MITSUBISHI
AUDIO TV VIDEO

IVECO OFFICIAL CLUB SPONSOR

Liverpool
Football League Division One
Saturday, 14 May 1983
Kick-off 3.00 p.m.
Programme 40p

20

The Chairman and Trustees of
The Anfield Foundation
have pleasure in inviting

Mr & Mrs Paisley

to the

Trophy Room at Anfield

on Wednesday 20th April 1988 at 7.45 p.m.
for the presentation of Awards by

Major General M.F. Hobbs C.B.E.
The Director of the Duke of Edinburghs' Award

R.S.V.P. - CHIEF EXECUTIVE
Monks Ferry, Church St., Birkenhead L41 5EG. Tel: 051-666 1470

Guests must produce this invitation on arrival

The final pictures . . .

Bob would often visit members of his family on day trips from Arncliffe Court Nursing Home, where he stayed for the final 14 months of his life as his Alzheimer's worsened. He would sit in the garden, just like he always did, enjoying a cup of tea and spending time with the grandchildren he loved. It was on one such occasion that the family took their last photos of him.

On a summer's day in 1995, with a hat to protect him from the hot sun, he smiled as he sat on a deckchair in son Graham's garden.

Although his memory was fading, there was one aspect of his life that never left him.

Jessie takes up the story . . .

The one thing he never forgot was his football. I remember the last time he was in one of our houses in Woolton.

We had brought him home for the day from the nursing home. We sat outside in the garden. His grandchild Rachael was out there and she started kicking a ball to him.

All the other senses had gone but he was kicking it back properly.

That was amazing.

These days, it's not a case of me missing him. It's more about remembering him. We have so many memories around us and in that respect we are very lucky. We have all those souvenirs to remind us of a wonderful man.

. . . and the game he never forgot

An ordinary man,
an extraordinary life

The Paisley collection of treasures that is spread far and wide among the family is remarkable.

Mementoes of historic European victories sit side by side with gifts from supporters' clubs and letters and photos sent by fans. The scrapbooks are the same. On the same page of cuttings telling the story of yet another trophy arriving on the Anfield sideboard are invitations to local fetes and thank you letters.

It is well documented that the famous Liverpool philosophy on which they built their success is that once you have won one cup, you start thinking about how you will lift the next. His simple footballing beliefs and the ethos of the Bootroom, where glorious campaigns were plotted over cups of tea and a cosy chat were integral to how he lived his life.

From tough times growing up in a North East mining village to his final years, he confronted each challenge head on, applying his own unshakeable set of values. He took each success and failure as it came, treating each imposter the same. The university degrees of his grandchildren would sit happily alongside a glittering European trophy. A family photo would be framed and mounted next to a glorious scene from another famous footballing conquest. Ultimately, it was this human quality in the midst of superhuman success that makes Paisley such a unique hero and one that should be celebrated – not least because he wouldn't celebrate his achievements himself.

When he died in 1996, a newspaper headline stood out to the family as they searched for a way to sum up the remarkable life of a loved one who emerged from humble beginnings to become the greatest British football manager of all time. Written as the headline to a front page article in the Times, it simply read . . .

'He remained an ordinary man amid extraordinary achievements.'

Son Graham takes up the story . . .

The headline was in the Times, they led on it. We used that and then Canon John Roberts used it in his sermon at the funeral. They were simple words but quite expressive.

He was a modest man. It's things like his war medals that sum it up. They have still been left in the original box, not that they didn't mean anything to him.

There is a saying that nice guys are not always successful. He probably did rub a few people up the wrong way but he was generally liked by most people. Ultimately his legacy is the trophies that he won.

My Mum has to take some credit in that she supported him throughout and made sure that whatever happened, our home life was normal.

Paisley's trophies raised Liverpool's expectations. He took the club on a journey beyond their wildest dreams, building on the platform left to him by his close friend and managerial mentor Bill Shankly. Recent years have seen the re-emergence of the club as a major European force. Graham says that his father would have been proud of the events of May 25, 2005, when another European Cup was added to Bob's three and the one won by Joe Fagan in Rome in 1984. Graham continues . . .

He was always of the opinion that things must move on. He would be pleased. The legacy of my Dad and the great '70s teams is that Liverpool are still getting players who are aware that Liverpool were THE team back then. Even the foreign players know Liverpool has that history.

In recent years when you go to the games, especially the European games, the atmosphere stands comparison with anything from the past. It has been recreated. There have been a few dark years but the Chelsea games have been as good as anything.

*Ultimately, though, the final word goes to the loyal wife who
stood behind him through an amazing life.
Her image of the Real Bob Paisley is a simple one . . .*

*'He was just an ordinary man.
We never thought of him as anything else.
To me, he was just 'My Bob'.
To the children, he was just Dad'*

– Jessie Paisley

Bob Paisley Honours

PAISLEY MANAGERIAL RECORD WITH LIVERPOOL

	P	W	D	L	F	A
League	378	212	99	67	648	294
FA Cup	36	20	7	9	62	27
League Cup	53	32	13	8	98	31
Europe	61	39	11	11	140	49
*Charity Shield	5	4	1	0	6	1
World Club	1	0	0	1	0	3
TOTAL	534	308	130	96	954	404

* Discounts 1974 Charity Shield

PAISLEY MANAGERIAL HONOURS

First Division champions (6)	1975-76, 1976-77, 1978-79, 1979-80, 1981-82, 1982-83
First Division runners-up	1974-75, 1977-78
FA Cup runners-up	1976-77
League Cup winners (3)	1980-81, 1981-82, 1982-83
League Cup runners-up	1977-78
FA Charity Shield winners (4)	1976, 1979, 1980, 1982
FA Charity Shield shared (1)	1977,
European Cup winners (3)	1976-77, 1977-78, 1980-81
UEFA Cup winners (1)	1975-76
European Super Cup winners (1)	1977-78
European Super Cup runners-up	1978-79
World Club runners-up	1981

PAISLEY REMAINS THE ONLY MAN IN HISTORY TO COACH 3 EUROPEAN CUP-WINNING SIDES.
PAISLEY WAS THE FIRST ENGLISH-BORN MANAGER TO WIN THE EUROPEAN CUP.

PAISLEY WON 6 MANAGER OF THE YEAR AWARDS:
1975-76 1976-77 1978-79 1979-80 1981-82 1982-83
HE ALSO WON THREE FIRST DIVISION MANAGER AWARDS AND TWO SPECIAL TROPHIES
MANAGER OF THE MONTH (At April 12, 1983):
1975 – December 1976 – April 1977 – March, April 1978 – February 1979 – December 1981 – April
1982 – January, March, November 1983 – January, March
IN ALL PAISLEY WOULD SCOOP 22 BELL'S MANAGERIAL AWARDS.
BOB WON 10 CHAMPIONSHIP WINNERS' MEDALS IN HIS VARIOUS ANFIELD ROLES.

BOB WAS GIVEN THE FREEDOM OF THE CITY OF LIVERPOOL, AND GRANTED AN O.B.E.
HE WAS GIVEN AN HONORARY DEGREE OF MASTER OF SCIENCE BY LIVERPOOL UNIVERSITY IN 1983
("I regard this as a particularly great honour. My wife is a schoolteacher and she is especially thrilled.")
APRIL 1983 ALSO SAW THE MAN COLLECT THE LIVERPOOL PUBLICITY ASSOCIATION GOLD MEDAL
(awarded to the person who has done most to promote Merseyside or improve the quality of life in the region).

PAISLEY WAS INDUCTED INTO THE ENGLISH FOOTBALL HALL OF FAME IN 2002.
IN NOVEMBER 1983 BOB WAS ONE OF 11 PEOPLE TO RECEIVE 'MEN OF THE YEAR' AWARDS
AT LONDON'S SAVOY HOTEL.

After scooping the Bell's Manager of the Month award for January 1982, Paisley set up a new record. It was his 16th such award, including manager of the season and special awards. The 16 gallon bottles contained 3,072 tots of whiskey. By December he had scooped the monthly prize a record 19 times.

Other titles produced by Sport Media:

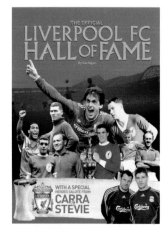

The Official Liverpool FC
Hall of Fame hardback (£20.00)
ISBN: 9781905266203

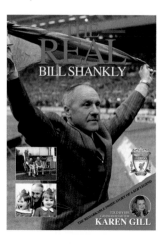

The Real Bill Shankly
(Now in paperback – £14.99)
ISBN: 9781905266500

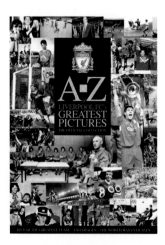

A-Z of Liverpool FC's Greatest
Pictures hardback (£20.00)
ISBN: 9781905266012

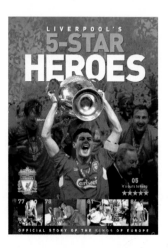

Liverpool's 5-Star Heroes
hardback (£20.00)
ISBN: 9781905266050

Subject to availability, these titles can be ordered by calling 0845
143 0001; by writing to Sport Media Books, PO Box 48, Old Hall
Street, L69 3EB or by logging on to www.merseyshop.com